WILDFOWLING
One Winter's Tale

WILDFOWLING
One Winter's Tale

ALAN JARRETT

DICKSON PRICE PUBLISHERS

Dickson Price Publishers
Hawthorne House
Bowdell Lane
Brookland
Kent TN29 9RW

First published 1988
© A. Jarrett

British Library Cataloguing in Publication Data

Jarrett, Alan
    Wildfowling.
    1.   Great Britain. Game birds. Shooting –
    Personal observations
    I.   Title
    799.2′4′0924

ISBN 0–907827–15–2

Set by R. H. Services, Welwyn, Hertfordshire
Printed and bound in Great Britain by
Biddles Ltd, Guildford and King's Lynn

Contents

Acknowledgements

Sincere thanks to Dee Martin who worked so hard translating my manuscript into neat typescript with such speed and precision, with scarcely a word of complaint.

I owe an enormous debt to friend and fellow Kent wildfowler Ian Phipps who drew the delightful line drawings and painted the picture for the cover of this book. How fortunate for me to find a man with such a feel for the Kentish marshes, such a love for the environment which we both know so well and a man with such a creative gift. I truly believe that Ian has a great future as a wildfowl artist.

Finally a big thank you to Eric Philp, keeper of the natural history section at Maidstone Museum who accorded me the facility to obtain the identification photographs which feature so prominently in what follows. Those who read the notes which accompany the identification photographs will do well to seek out and study any local museum collection – for no photograph or drawing can possibly do justice to such a subject. If you live within hailing distance of Maidstone in Kent you will be hard put to find a more fulsome or better display.

No doubt many provincial museums possess such fine collections and bird enthusiasts will find the visit worthwhile both aesthetically and educationally. Purely by chance the Maidstone collection was mostly presented by another wildfowler in 1946 – Guy Mannering; most of his collection was obtained in Kent and Sussex, and he mounted his first specimen at the age of 16. Guy Mannering lived from 1881–1966.

Introduction

Wildfowling, perhaps more than any other of our shooting sports, is heavily steeped in tradition and romanticisms. This is not a product of the writer's pen, but exists as a result of the possibly unique affection which wildfowlers feel for both shore and their elusive quarry; the shores and estuaries are as wild an environment as one could wish to find within the UK, and inspire men to pit their wits against the birds which live there. In this book I have attempted to capture some of that essential wildness of the shore, to convey the sportsman's reverence for his quarry and to condense the magic of the sport into a few brief chapters. At the same time I have attempted to inform – in a light sort of way – so that which follows is a mixture of practical information and anecdote, and is, I hope, a recreation of one man's sport that will both instruct and entertain.

The concept of the hunter/naturalist/conservationist is an apparent paradox, the like of which few sportsmen will have come across before. How can he who loves wild creatures and their wild environment so very dearly be so willing to hunt and kill? All too frequently that question will be asked, and not unreasonably I feel. I write these pages in order to better explain the sport of wildfowling to those who do not yet understand, and in so doing readily admit that it is no easy task!

As a child, a youth and finally a young man, I was brought up in the countryside, with Nature and her creatures all around me every minute of every day. I was taught to love and value Nature, and that modest harvest of the bountiful countryside was no bad thing. It is therefore scarcely surprising that I should allow the natural environment to form such a prominent place in my thoughts and actions over the years; nor surprising that I should find the environment increasingly fascinating as time passed by. To anyone who takes more than a fleeting interest in what goes on around them this last statement will come as no surprise at all – the more one learns, the more one finds there is to be learnt.

So in many ways this love of the countryside was to shape my life; so too did my pursuit of that harvest mentioned earlier, via fieldsports – shooting in the main. By carrying a gun and hunting wild creatures I learned how to come to intimate terms with my quarry, and in so doing probably learned more about Nature than many of a comparable age. It was essential that I acquired such a detailed knowledge if I were to become a successful shooting man.

To somebody brought up away from the coast it is perhaps a little curious that this environment held such a fascination for me: to me nothing could compare with the desperate wildness to be found on those vast, uninhabited tracts of saltings and marshland adjacent to the sea. There on the marshes and foreshores was a real wildness which invaded my blood from the very first time I laid eyes upon it.

It was a natural extension of my shooting experience that I should be drawn to the coast to shoot; to shoot wildfowl, and attempt to experience some of the magic which was reputedly attached to this branch of the sport. The magic of these places completely captivated me; the smell of the saltmarshes; the quarry, and the other wildfowlers that plied their trade over this wild land. As my love for wildfowling increased so my involvement in other forms of the sport was bound to wane. Very soon I was not content unless I could hear the waves rolling onto some muddy beach, and the excited calling of the wild birds. Even in the early formative years, when my sport was inevitably relatively unsuccessful, I gladly sacrificed my other sport – for even then I could find no real substitute for wildfowling.

All too quickly the years have passed, and so my involvement in the sport has grown; now every facet of the sport and the coast fascinates me, making me eager to gain extra knowledge. Now I feel I can use that knowledge to make a positive contribution in return for the harvest to which I feel entitled. The study of the coast would take a lifetime, and yet still remain far from complete – but I can think of few worthier causes to devote one's time to! Winter-time here in the South-East of England is by far the most spectacular time of the year, for this is when the thronging multitudes of migrant birds are with us having fled the onset of winter on the far northern breeding grounds. This is the time of year when ornithologist and wildfowler alike can benefit the most. Lucky is the man who is ornithologist and wildfowler rolled into one, for he will reap the greatest reward of all. I have now reached the stage where I clearly recognise that I am in love with the coast first, and with the sport secondly – the fact that the two can go hand in hand is fortunate indeed. It is my love for the coast which has inspired these pages, and thankfully I see little sign that this emotion will abate.

To the experienced and dedicated wildfowler there is no need to explain the fascination which grips us all; but for those that are not captivated by the wildfowling fever much explanation will be needed, yet even then there can be no possible substitute for actually going down to the shore itself. What do such people see when confronted with the shore? They see endless acres of ostensibly lifeless mud and saltmarsh; then sense the danger of the tide and the clinging mud, but above all they feel the cold wind that chills them to the marrow. They see little to attract them.

But what does the wildfowler see? The chapters which follow will elaborate, but briefly – he sees the coast through rose-coloured spectacles: he sees the marshes teeming with wildlife, be it hare or wildfowl, quartering raptor or stationary heron, for the coast is far from the emptiness seen by the untrained eye. Wildfowling presents the sort of challenge which is all too often sadly lacking in a modern stereo-typed society. It is the cold and danger, and the inherent hardships which go to make it the thrilling sport which it is; he who can face the biting cold of a winter's day and the menace of a creeping tide, and still come away with a bird or two in the bag, can walk proud indeed.

The experienced wildfowler becomes a part of the coast over which he hunts his quarry. Not for him the outlandish seawall-prowling activities of the gaudily dressed pseudo-ornithologists; rather he will be dressed in somber hues, and be

ensconsed unobtrusively amongst the aster and *spartina* of the saltmarsh. He will be able to observe without being seen, and thus learn all the quicker; surely such an attitude is as vital for successful ornithology as it is for successful wildfowling. Many writers have conveyed their own evocative descriptions of the marshes onto the page, and by so doing doubtless hope to enthrall and captivate the reader; we mostly differ in how we see the coast, and in what is considered the most poignant reminder of these wild places. For me it is always the pungent smell, which contributes so readily to the 'feel' of the place; it is a curious mix of acrid muds, of rotting vegetation and flotsam, and of salt. There is nothing else quite like it. To he who becomes addicted to the coasts, and to contact with the wildfowl which inhabit such places, there can be no substitute: periods spent inland are absolute torture, whilst those periods spent on the coast will be sheer bliss. The true wildfowler can 'see' the coast, even when he is many miles away – the only inspiration necessary being a gust of chill wind.

During one May we were in the opening throes of what turned out to be a long, wet summer. The wind blew out of the north-east and there was a chill in the air reminiscent of colder days – one could so easily have been forgiven for thinking it was winter. It was then that I realised that I had to set my thoughts down on paper. 60 yards from the window where I sat to write these first words stands a magnificent copper beech tree. For over a week these cold winds blew and a big moon rode high in the night sky – yes, it could so easily have been November. Whilst the dog took her nightly stroll I stood and shivered in my shirt-sleeves; all was silent save for the wind whispering through the surrounding fields of barley and through the branches of the copper beech – it was a glorious feeling.

On one particular evening, when the moon was almost full, the wind stirred the copper beech mightily. There was that intense goose-pimpling chill in the air; white clouds raced all across the night sky, and my thoughts fled back to the saltings and to those many moonlight flights which I have enjoyed there. For several minutes I was completely captivated. Was that the shrill whistle of an approaching pack of wigeon? Was there a far off hint of goose music? No. It was all in my imagination. How I longed for the new season to begin, so that I could once again enjoy such sounds. I write so that others might share something of that enjoyment, and savour some of the special magic of the coast. Perhaps, if I have done this job well, others might also hurry to the shore, and in this manner our sport will live on forever.

—1—

Opening Day

WILDFOWLING IS OF course an exclusively winter sport. But where does winter begin and end? Where does autumn fit into the great scheme of things?

For the wildfowler summer ends, at long last, at midnight on the last day of August – and winter begins in that same instant. His winter lifestyle will begin as the first streaks of dawn light the eastern sky on that first morning of September; he will have no time to concern himself with the refinements of the seasons, for autumn will have little meaning for him. Not that autumn will be dismissed lightly or contemptuously. To many this is the finest season of the year – and who is to say that this is not so? Yet there are few reminders that autumn is with us when on the shore, so the tendency is to disregard its official presence. To the wildfowler winter begins on September First and ends on February 20 – official seasons count for nought!

All summer long the wildfowler will have fretted his way through torrid heat, and agonisingly long daylight hours; perhaps interspersed with occasional trips to the shore to see how things are progressing. But the shore in summer is mostly a drab, uninspiring sort of place, where the grasses grow high and harbour an irritating multitude of biting insects, whilst the fertile muds are virtually devoid of bird life. Yet the winds, be they ever so gentle, are still there to serve as a reminder of wilder winter days. The wildfowl, perhaps tamer and less plentiful than during winter months, are enough to make the heart beat faster and, if the flocks are of any size come mid-August, there is plenty of theorising that perhaps this year the early part of the season will be that much better than average.

The wildfowler is one of life's great optimists and planners. With good reason too, for the sport is apt to throw up disappointments with almost astonishing regularity! Were he not an optimist, the wildfowler would soon abandon the sport in favour of another likely to offer greater material reward. A planner because of the many complex permutations governing his sport, such as wind and tide and moon, and, of course, actual time of year. The fact that often his optimism proves ill-founded and misplaced matters little, nor the fact that even the most meticulous planning is likely to end in failure on the majority of occasions seems to deter the true enthusiast for more than a moment. Yes, wildfowlers are a strange breed; a race apart, perhaps throwbacks to another age.

As August draws toward its close there is much to be done, with a state of near-hysteria building up as the season approaches. For the newcomer the task of preparation may seem almost beyond him unaided, whilst for the older hand this is a ritual which causes few problems; yet the excitement never wanes, and when it does wane this will surely be time to turn elsewhere for recreation. The season rushes ever closer and, as always, there is so much to be done and so little time in which to do it. But no matter how much feverish preparation there is to be carried out, there will still remain enough time for some delightful reminiscence of flights now long gone.

Planning and preparation

My shooting diary is a crucially important part of my life, for without its prompting I would lose many precious and irreplaceable memories. As the season draws near it is a delight to laze by the hearth and thumb through the pages yet again, so that past glories might be relived and a greater sense of anticipation be enjoyed as a result. From the pages of the diary I can recall flights from long ago, with perhaps nothing more than a few perfunctory comments to ignite the spark of memory; now I can recall some special flight, or a spectacular shot, as though it happened only brief moments before. The pages come alive: the cold wind seems to chill right through me; one can almost hear the tearing of teal wings as they rend the air, whilst the wild yodel of goose music may come surging up from the open page. The maps and tide tables are of enormous importance as aids to various plottings and schemings and gloatings. The fact that few such plans reach fruition is of little consequence, for this is all part of the pre-season hysteria! But he who fails to keep a diary of sorts robs himself of many hours of nostalgic enjoyment in the future, and this is one way of softening the blow occasioned by the close seasons' loss of sport.

The newcomer will need maps of the locality in which he intends to operate: ordnance survey map, plus any maps made available by the club to which so many of today's wildfowlers belong. A current tide table will also be a necessity, whilst learning to relate its predictions to the area which will be the scene of operations may seem an elementary requirement, but one surprisingly disregarded by many. If he has acted wisely the newcomer will have been down to the shore in August to check out the details shown on his maps. Access routes and parking places should have been learnt, for these can be the very devil in the gloom of some dawnflight period; similarly the walk out to the marsh should be learnt, and tramped over in order to find any potential trouble spots such as deep creeks or rickety bridges which may provoke near-heart failure in the dark.

August is the time to study the tides in relation to the tide table, in order to identify which parts of the marsh flood easily, and which parts – if any – may act as a haven on the larger tides which will inevitably inundate much of the saltmarsh. Out of season there will be less urgency involved, and one can learn the marsh at one's leisure, rather than at the behest of some murderous flood tide! The planning and preparation stage must be carried out in a thorough and meticulous manner if later inconvenience is to be avoided; in an extreme case the consequences of any error at this time can be dire indeed, with more than one sportsman paying the supreme penalty for a momentary lapse of memory! My car boot, which doubles nicely as a mobile garden shed, will need a good clear out to allow room for the piles of wildfowling equipment, with the medley of summer shooting accessories being discarded for at least the next six months. Then the wildfowling gear which has been tucked away out of sight, if scarcely forgotten, will need to be brought out for inspection, with possible replacement or repair before it is once again ready to meet the demands of the foreshore.

Be properly equipped
Wildfowling is a complex and arduous sport, and in order to operate efficiently the sportsman will need to be comprehensively equipped. The newcomer will find the initial financial outlay considerable although, thankfully, most items will need replacement but seldom, and rarely will more than a single piece of equipment need renewal at a time. Even on the balmiest of September days the foreshore can be a wet and muddy place, inclined to wreck and ruin unprotected clothing; the wildfowler will need full combat gear if he is to keep both dry and clean, so that, broadly speaking, the same equipment will last the season

Some of the equipment needed for a day on the saltmarsh.

through. Admittedly, some wildfowlers prefer a lightweight coat for early season sport, but I avoid most of those sweaty walks by carrying my coat in a rucksack, most certainly I find this better than ruining two coats instead of one. So, the mandatory waders, or thigh boots, must be checked for leaks; waterproof trousers and coats for leaks and tears, with repair and reproofing where necessary. Cartridge belts and bags similarly checked over, whilst the gun slip will need to be serviceable for at least the start of the season. Ideally, the gun slip should be of some cheap canvas or PVC material, as mine doubles for a rudimentary seat when in the saltings – at least some protection from cold mud/salting against ill-protected backside is most desirable, and will act as a deterrent for the various ailments associated with prolonged freezing of the nether regions!

I shall deal with guns and cartridges elsewhere. Suffice to say that a wildfowler's gun is apt to bear a rather battered appearance after a number of seasons use, for no conditions are more ruinous of metal than that of the salt-laden foreshore. On return from flight, speedy and thorough cleaning will be necessary if the worse effects of mud and water are to be kept at bay. A pre-season checkover by a gunsmith may prove to be money well spent, and may avoid inconvenient breakdowns during the weeks and months ahead. The wildfowler's dog will also be referred to later in this book, but nobody should underestimate for a moment the vital importance of such a companion. A trained dog (often a very loose term to attach to a wildfowling dog) can make all the difference when in a gloomy twilight world of mud and water and tangled saltmarsh, and few serious sportsmen will be without one for very long. Even a dead bird can be the very devil to retrieve from the saltmarsh, whilst a wounded bird might test even the best of dogs, giving the dogless wildfowler virtually no chance.

As will be seen throughout this book, the wildfowler's first duty is to his quarry, indeed this is something which all shooting sportsmen worthy of the name must consider as their top priority. To the non-wildfowler, the wildfowler's deep regard, even love, for his quarry is a crazy paradox with which they are unable to come to terms, or to find any parallel; but wildfowlers are a special type of shooting man, whose quarry and hunting conditions are also quite unique. A love for one's quarry is not some wild hypocrisy, rather a statement of respect, even awe. Having decided to take the life of another living creature the sportsman must be obliged to do so in as swift and competent a manner as he possibly can. Having shot the creature it must be retrieved without delay, and thereafter, if still alive, despatched instantly and humanely. Although we sport for birds and animals we must do so within the confines just outlined, and can scarcely attract much discredit so long as we obey these simple commonsense criteria. Everything which I describe henceforth is geared towards this end – the efficient pursuance of sport without cruelty and resultant dishonour.

What of the other aids to wildfowling? Check the wading pole is still sound; that the compass is still in working order; if a boat is to be used, it and all its ancilliary equipment must be given the once over; the rucksack, for carrying decoys, the slain birds and other items, must be checked for rotten or broken straps. The list is long. The decoys, so important on occasions, will need attention: see that they still float upright, that anchor weights and lines are secure, and that any white signal patches are still bright and clear, whilst a touch up with some white matt paint will enhance the overall effect of the 'flock'. More of decoys later. Almost ready for the off – only the actual flighting place remains a mystery perhaps. This is where the diary, maps and tide table will play their crucial part, for the experienced wildfowler will already have an inkling of where he intends to spend the first day of the season. Often the bag will be light, or even zero, but the moment is usually very special: yes, the first day of September heralds the start of another wildfowling campaign, and the majority of sportsmen will be down on the shore to sample its heady delights.

The Glorious First
The First is a traditional shooting day for wildfowlers, just as the Glorious Twelfth is for the grouse enthusiast. No matter what the bag, it is the chase which matters most. To attempt to describe the First adequately is perhaps a futile exercise, but it is well worth such an attempt, for in this manner it is possible to convey something of the flavour of a season which will stretch away before you for almost six months. The wildfowling season is a marathon affair, subject to many variations and changes throughout its considerable length. Here I include a description of two such opening days – one spent beside the seawall itself, with the second being of a more traditional nature spent on the foreshore.

Soon all the equipment is stowed away in the car; at last the sun is setting in the western sky and, as August 31 dies slowly away, I feel summer die with it. The time draws near, and winter is just a brief few hours away. What of the dog? Can the yellow labrador sense the coming of the new season, or is she simply reacting to the excitement which I exude? I can never know the answer to such a question, only that she is full of life and eager to be away.

We left, the dog and I, when it was still summer. It was far too early, but I found it impossible to rest, instead hoping for a little sleep in the car whilst awaiting the time to be away. The stabbing light from the headlights wove a crazy pattern as I negotiated the pot-holed track which winds down through the marsh, driving slowly from necessity as I value my car suspension – in any case there was no hurry. Once safely parked it was possible to relax a little. But it is never an easy matter to sleep in the uncomfortable confines of the car, a problem accentuated by the great moon, just past the full, which stared down into the car lighting up the interior almost like day. There was a distinct chill in the air which was quite impossible to shake, so I slept in snatches; but in all honesty it was the mounting anticipation as much as the cold which caused the sleeplessness.

I woke with a start to find another car parked close by, and as I had not detected its arrival concluded that perhaps I had enjoyed more sleep than I had at first thought. A glance at the watch told me that it was almost one o'clock on the first day of winter; now sleep was forgotten as other like-minded men were close by, and there would be so much to discuss before it was time to head off to

Sheltered fleet with abundant club rush.

pre-determined flighting places. One of the great delights of this sport is the fact that it is possible to engage in earnest conversation with those who are no more than casual acquaintances. We sat out in the moonlight, drinking sharp-tasting, sugarless black coffee and speculating on what the season ahead might hold; it was a time to swap tales of past days, and was an altogether pleasant interlude. Soon others arrived. We were all friends in a fashion, and willing enough to swap yarns and pleasantries, but at the same time we were all guarded in what was said. At this late hour it was important not to give too much away, and before too long I slipped away into the night – eager to be alone and on my way to the chosen place.

I had a long walk, which mattered very little as there was still plenty of time before dawn broke. In many places the marsh was bathed in low, swirling mist, which draped itself like some vague, ghostly shawl wherever a hollow was to be found – scarcely inspiring wildfowling weather, even if it was fairly typical of the First. By the time I reached the end of my stumbling walk the rucksack seemed to have doubled in weight; my shirt felt sticky across my shoulders where the sweat had rubbed beneath the straps, and it was blessed relief to shed the load. The sound of mallard departing from the shallow water of the fleet was music to my ears, and a few moments later their ghostly silhouettes crossed the light beneath the moon – then they were gone. The decoys were set out in the shallows and the gun loaded; thereafter it was just a case of waiting for the sky to begin to pale in the east, and for the first duck to appear. Just a few short yards away out on the fore-shore the tide was remorselessly flooding the flats, pushing the waders before it; those spirit voices of the shore – the curlew, grey plover and redshank – complained bitterly at this intrusion, just as they did on every tide. A deep contentment settled over me – it was so good to be back.

The first duck of that new season came out of the rapidly paling eastern sky, a pack of whispery-winged mallard, too high and wide for a first shot. Even as I considered the mallard, a single teal came in quickly, to plough up the surface of the fleet as it landed, to be swiftly followed by a second then a third; this third bird offered an easy chance as it planed down amongst the decoys, but for some inexplicable reason I did not fire. The three of them sat there and regarded their surroundings with grave suspicion, so that when I showed myself they were off in a flash. An initial hesitation proved my undoing, for the single shot was totally ineffective!

More duck began to criss-cross the morning sky, mostly too far away to warrant a shot, although twice swiftly-flying packs of teal provoked unsuccessful attempts. Finally I cut a teal out to a very respectable shot; the dog retrieved the little bird with great alacrity, and the first bird of the season was in the bag. Soon enough the reassuring decoys and my seductive calling lured another teal to the gun, for it to fall into the reed- filled shallows with a broken wing. A wounded teal is a stern challenge for any dog under such circumstances, and the hunt was long and loud before a very proud dog presented me with the tiny duck. A fine piece of dog work. High flying mallard, one of which I managed to bring down, plus a few shoveler, served to keep me alert and, although I have often seen more birds on the First, there was still a good showing. A moratorium on wader shooting benefited various species, especially the snipe of which there were plenty; in fact these tiny long-billed birds were bold in the extreme, constantly skimming the reed tops or flying very low overhead – their rasping calls providing a perfect backcloth to the morning's sport.

It is the voices of wildfowl and waders which contribute so substantially to the atmosphere of the marshes. This morning other birds came to the fleet, so that there was a medley of differing calls to enthrall me and make me doubly glad to be back: redshank, greenshank and spotted redshank all came, whilst a few curlew flew

The cold light of a grey dawn over the flats.

sedately into the marshes to feed. A thoroughly wonderful morning. Three very low mallard gave me an easy chance, but I dragged the shot somehow so that the target bird carried on for fully 100 yards before falling into a nightmare tangle of browning marsh grasses. It took more excellent work by the dog to bring this fine bird to hand; he was a big drake, just coming out of eclipse plumage, with his crop stuffed full of barley gleaned from the harvest.

Thus the morning flight was over, and I made my weary way back to the car. The others were all there, all seemingly cheery enough, irrespective of the size of their bag, for the season lay ahead like some massive test of endurance and there would be plenty of sport to come. For my part I had killed four fine birds, even if I had missed quite a few in the process, and was therefore more than happy with the result of my efforts. Now I needed rest above all else before the evening flight – for the call of the marsh was strong. So four birds taken on the opening morning in fairly clean and straight-forward circumstances. Close to the shore, yet far enough away to lose some of that essential essence of the sport; no mud or danger of any type, and scarcely wildfowling to the purist. Shooting away from the shore itself is really duck shooting as opposed to wildfowling, even if it is a very enjoyable pastime.

Seldom have I spent the First in such surroundings, mostly wallowing on the shore in various places with varying degrees of success. Usually a bird in the bag is reward enough, whilst three–five duck can be considered fairly good by any standards. Only once in my wildfowling 'career' to date have I put together a really good bag on opening day and it is worth recording here as an example of the one-off fluke we all dream of, yet seldom attain.

A perfect opening day

That August I had not bothered much with reconnaissance, for I had pre-judged where I wanted to flight, and knew from experience that this was likely to produce a bird or two. Only the season before I had shot four duck at morning flight, with little effort, so that the chances of a repeat performance were enough to make up my mind without too much of the usual fretting and worry. The only possible fly in the ointment was the activities of other wildfowlers, on whom I had to steal a march if I was to be certain of getting what I considered to be the prime position. Really the state of the tide made my mind up for me, for it was a late afternoon/early morning high tide. Having decided, mainly for convenience, to use my punt for access this left me with two choices: to arrive on the salting pre-dawn on the First, in which case the majority of the most likely flighting positions would already be occupied, or to go up on the afternoon flood on the 31, necessitating a full night out on the salting but with a chance of picking my spot.

I chose the later course of action, and it proved to be a wise choice for only one other wildfowler – a fine old chap of long acquaintance – was in position. I punted down the wide, semi-flooded creek and positioned myself slightly to his north; an hour later, at the top of the tide, a larger boat came in and anchored to my north, thus this small piece of salting was nicely occupied. Twice on that tide other wildfowlers punted in, and had to make for other parts, so that if I had gone up on the morning tide I should have missed out altogether. My older friend had a bigger boat moored in the channel, and commuted by dingy to the salting. He had erected a rudimentary hide, more as a way of staking his claim than anything else, and he soon came over for a long and enjoyable chin-wag. Yes, he had seen a big flight through when he arrived on the previous afternoon, and he confidently predicted that this was the place to be. The sense of anticipation for the morrow was building nicely. At high water I dragged the punt from the water and covered it over. Inside I had an inflatable mattress, and the erection of a canvas awning would serve to keep both dew and mosquitoes at bay as I was determined to see in the First in something like a normal state of health.

As the tide began to ebb the mallard started flighting off to the east, no doubt to glean from the stubbles which lay in profusion at the back of the marshes. They came right over the salting I had chosen, and seldom have I seen such a flight. For some two hours the sky was filled with packs of mallard, few of which were too high to shoot at – it was an incredible sight. At length, as the first stars began to appear in the cloudless void above, I lay back in the punt and listened to the sighing of their wings, whilst every now and again a low pack would race overhead. Surely, I reasoned, if this flight was to be repeated on the morrow I should have one of the best flights of my life; no, it could not happen, as the earlier shooting at morning flight was bound to disperse the birds. My mind was filled with such confused thoughts. What of the morning flight? If this great throng of birds returned on the same line it would be some flight.

My early plans had entailed morning flight, with my departure on the first of the afternoon tide, though I was now in a quandary about the best course of action for to leave on the flood would mean missing the evening flight. An interesting series of questions to occupy my excited brain as I settled down to sleep. In truth this was probably the best sleep I have ever had on the saltings, and I awoke before dawn refreshed and incredibly excited. Yet for all that, the still morning air caused me to shudder as a chill settled over me, everything was covered in dew and the lack of wind was scarcely stimulating. Strangely the huge mallard flight did not materialise that morning, so they must have mostly gone back to their roost during the early hours as we all slept. There was little shooting on the saltmarsh, but I did very well to get four plump mallard, whilst scarcely another duck was killed.

The long between-flights period of the First is mostly a boring time, no matter how hard one tries to keep some enthusiasm going. The weather was very hot, making me very tired, whilst scarcely a bird moved. Admittedly one can pass the time of day with other sportsmen, and very enjoyable this can be, but the wait for the evening flight is seemingly endless. At length the tide was surging past me along the big creek. Now the dilemma – to leave well satisfied with a modest bag or to remain in the hope that the big flight would develop with the onset of evening? The deciding factor was the relatively poor morning flight – I believed the birds had not been greatly disturbed. Yes, I would stay, even though this might cause me difficulties in getting the punt out of the draining creek. The day before the flight had begun with the ebb tide, but I was tucked into a tiny creek ready and waiting long before that, just in case. Nothing moved, though I noted the gradual disappearance of other sportsmen, until the great saltmarsh was almost empty save for the three of us faithfully and optimistically lining the anticipated line of flight; doubtless this was testimony to the general lack of sport enjoyed at the morning flight, so that few were sufficiently inspired to see the day out.

A snipe sneaked around the edge of the seawall and I killed it as it crossed the salting. The dog retrieved it smoothly to hand, comically presenting the bird as a tail and long bill protruding from opposite sides of the mouth. Once in hand I noted the dampness of its delicately camouflaged brown plumage from the warm interior of the dog's mouth. The tide slopped into the saltings, flooding all the tiny creeks, though not high enough to reach the top or make things uncomfortable. This is a quiet time on the shore, for most of the waders are off to some comfortable roost, with only the occasional redshank or small flock of dunlin to be seen, as though on scouting duties waiting for the tide to turn so that they can get down to the urgent business of feeding once again on the uncovering muds.

Right on cue, just after high water, the first pack of mallard appeared, heading purposefully for my position. I took the shot over my left shoulder and the dead bird hit the salting with a satisfying thump. This was the start of a procession of birds coming straight to me as if on rails, with the added bonus coming in the form of me shooting remarkably straight. Mostly the birds were fairly low, sometimes disappearing below the seawall as they approached before flying into my field of fire. Of the higher packs one bird stands out in the memory as being taken above the point of my right shoulder – it seemed to fall for an age before hitting the water with the most enormous and satisfying of splashes. The dog was working well, even if most retrieves were of a fairly simple nature anyway. A longish shot out to my left killed a single bird, which brought warranted chastisement from my friend who claimed that it was his bird. I left the next pair, and he missed them both barrels! A few minutes later another pair crossed between us and I downed them both with a crisp pair of shots, and thankfully he said nothing further.

A single tall bird, which crashed dead into the creek, turned out to be a young common pochard, and this bird was to prove the only variation to my bag of mallard which was building nicely. Still the duck came straight to me, whilst any that deviated straightened delightfully at my call. The Guns to my right and left were hardly firing a shot, and the experience was quite remarkable. Another downed pair created a problem as they were both in the water. The dog brought the dead bird, whilst the second swam off out of sight up a side creek from which it would prove difficult to collect. In the end the punt was cast afloat and a few strokes of the paddle took me in search of the missing bird; how adept at concealment are these birds, for it was tucked under an overhang of sea purslane and did not flinch when I passed within three feet of it. I had to avoid putting it back into the water at all costs, for a diving mallard in a deep creek is not my idea of fun. So long as it believed itself hidden it would stay where it was, and that suited me perfectly. By reversing the punt in close to the creek bank I was able to reach out and grab the bird before it could move, and once inboard I quickly despatched it.

By now the creek was fast emptying, the light was fading and the flight was drying up a little. The events of the First had obviously dissipated the mallard somewhat as there were fewer birds than had been evident during the previous afternoon; notwithstanding this it was still a very big flight indeed, and perhaps the best I had experienced to date. At length I decided to give it best, whilst I could still get out of the creek, even though there was still the likelihood of a shot or two. But as I had 10 mallard and the pochard to add to my four mallard from the morning flight, I considered that I had shot enough anyway. It had been one of those flights when I could do no wrong, and as such it will long remain as a high point in my wildfowling experience.

There was a bare finger of drab water in the creek bottom as I made my way out, more by pushing on the muddy banks than by actual paddling. The steep creek walls seemed grey and sinister in the fading light, whilst the vegetation atop was vague and spindly as it was silhouetted against the darkening sky; all was quiet save for my own progress, until I reached the main channel and struck out purposefully for home. The gulls complained from the mudflats around, whilst the odd curlew gave vent to its feelings with typical melodious whistle; far away I knew that the mallard legions were shovelling up the spilt grain, scarcely any the worse for my cull. I had made an exceptional bag by many standards but had not shot too many, with every bird picked and stowed in the nose of the punt for ultimate human consumption. This is the way it should be: strong-flying wild birds shot under sporting conditions, for later use on the table – without a morsel wasted.

It felt good to be alive then, alone with only the dog for company in the insular world of the punt; all around the blackness of the

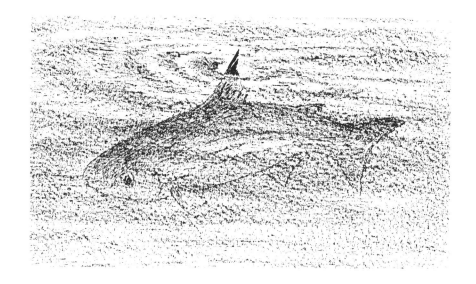

September night, the steady rush of water past the cleaving hull and the unhurried dip of my paddle into the inky water. To sport for wild birds in wild surroundings is a wonderful experience, but to succeed as a wildfowler is something extra. It is the picking up of the gauntletted challenge of life, and the overcoming of often mountainous odds. A good beginning to a new season.

—2—

A Blueprint for Sport

I SHOT MY FIRST wild duck in broad daylight one sunny afternoon on September 9 1968, on a small, rather scruffy marsh beside the river Medway in Kent. It was of course a mallard and I killed it with consummate ease using game load of number 6 shot. I was then 18-years-old and burning with a desire to become a wildfowler; a score of years later I can say that I have indeed become a wildfowler, and have killed many duck since that first afternoon. Perhaps with good fortune I shall still be hunting duck come the year 2008, thus doubling my present 20 sporting years.

In 1968 the *Firearms Act* came into being, and in many ways sounded the death knell for the lone-wolf wildfowler, even if I could not appreciate the fact at the time. Soon the willy-nilly meandering over the shore with a gun became a thing of the past, with syndicate or club membership gradually becoming a pre-requisite if one wished to enjoy any meaningful sport. Nevertheless there was still plenty of opportunity for sport, whilst the actual pursuance of the sport was largely unfettered by restrictions. Today the sport has changed out of all recognition, and sadly I have played my part, although I like to think that I have helped rescue the sport in Kent rather than being instrumental in imposing excessive restrictions.

Competition for land use for a host of recreational pursuits has been a prime reason for problems, whilst the commercialisation of wildfowling by some who should know better has also had a terribly damaging effect. But most tragic of all has been the introduction of the *Wildlife and Countryside Act 1981* which came into effect during September 1982. This must rank as the single biggest victory for protectionists since the *Protection of Birds Act 1954*, and was a set-back for wildfowlers unparalled in modern times. Truly the

The river miles inland – the spawning ground of many a wildfowler.

newcomers to the sport will not know any different, but I hereby attest that in some ways our sport has been devastated. It is a devastation from which it will never fully recover.

Admittedly there are still plenty of species for us to shoot and the list of those which may be taken in season is as follows:

Duck:	Mallard	*Geese:*	Greylag
	Wigeon		Pinkfoot
	Teal		Canada
	Pintail		European White-front
	Shoveler		
	Gadwall	*Waders:*	Golden Plover
	Tufted		Snipe
	Common Pochard		
	Goldeneye		

But the list of those lost during the passage of the *1981 Act* is also long, and most sadly of all includes almost all the waders. Most certainly the shooting of shore waders is now a thing of the past. Protected under the *1981 Act*:

Duck:	Garganey	*Waders:*	Curlew
	Long-tailed		Redshank
	Scaup		Grey Plover
	Common Scoter		Bar-tailed Godwit
	Velvet Scoter		Whimbrel
			Jack Snipe
Geese:	Bean		

Thankfully the seasons have been left unaltered: these being, for ducks, geese and waders September 1 – January 31 inclusive, whilst there remains the extra period on the foreshore – below high water mark of ordinary spring tides – until February 20 for the shooting of ducks and geese only.

How does this wildfowler view such changes? How do they affect the sport as we knew it? We must be objective in all things if we are to retain any creditability, and in many cases the list of newly-protected birds has not affected our sport greatly. The protection of the marine ducks – the scoters, long-tailed and scaup may have been a blow to a handful of punt-gunners and to more than a few of those shooting the Scottish firths, but for the average English wildfowler they represent virtually no loss at all. Personally I have only shot scaup in times of hard weather, and do not much care for the flesh of marine diving ducks anyway. However, I do not condone protection on these grounds alone. The garganey is but a summer migrant, leaving during September, and once again represents no great loss, although one doubts that enough garganey have ever been shot to make much difference to population levels anyway. The bean goose is undoubtedly uncommon in Great Britain, although reasonably plentiful on the continent; its loss is probably negligible, but once again the number killed must have been minute. Perhaps in real terms the loss of ducks and bean goose is neither here nor there, though the principal involved is probably another matter. The sweeping loss of all the shore waders is quite another thing, but for the sake of objectivity it is as well to consider them individually.

Of all our sporting birds pre-1981, the jack snipe was probably the least challenging, indeed its suicidal habit of landing close by again once flushed was as good a reason for removing if from the quarry list as one could find. For the average foreshore wildfowler it would figure but seldom in the bag, although just what implications such protection had elsewhere I can scarcely comment.

As with the garganey, the whimbrel leaves these shores early in the season and figured only modestly in the bag. With both grey plover and bar-tailed godwit there will always be arguments for and against their protection; to me they were always good sporting birds well worthy of powder and shot and as palatable as any shore bird can be. But if their numbers were truly in decline all good wildfowlers would support the call for complete protection.

Which brings us to the curlew and redshank. To many sportsmen the other shore waders figured rarely in the bag, but for many curlew and redshank were an important part of their sport, especially during the relatively duckless days of September and early October. The damage to the breeding habitat of the redshank by changing agricultural practice can not be denied, and a short-term fall in numbers seems to be the case, but the species is still extremely numerous and protection has given rise to much resentment. The case of the curlew is an absolute outrage against the sportsman, and makes a mockery of scientific impartiality, for nowhere has there been shown a clear case for protection, indeed the Governments' Nature Conservancy Council, stated this at the time. Yet the curlew received protection because of parliamentary chicanery; subsequently all efforts by the British Association for Shooting and Conservation – the wildfowlers' parent body – to gain reinstatement of this species have met with failure; the NCC have fallen off the fence on the protectionist side, with the 'green' Minister William Waldegrave, disinclined to listen to the wild-fowlers' argument.

Many wildfowlers feel bitter at the needless protection of a plentiful and legitimate sporting quarry, and it will be a long time before we will trust the likes of the NCC again. Has the loss of the curlew done any lasting damage to the sport? How great is the loss to wildfowlers nationwide? The first question is more difficult to answer. Most certainly wader shooting during early season was never pursued by all wildfowlers; however, many tyros learnt the sport under fairly easy early-season conditions whilst hunting waders, and it was an excellent introduction to life on the shore. How many newcomers have been subsequently lost to the sport it is not possible to say, but there must surely have been some loss. The loss to sportsmen nationwide is considerable; once again not all wildfowlers shot curlew, but a substantial proportion did enjoy this marvellous sport and for a great many the loss has been a severe blow, and in extreme cases virtually decimated their sport for weeks at a time.

The *1981 Act* affected sport in other ways too, indeed the very basis of sport has totally altered in many instances. The comprehensive renotification of Sites of Special Scientific Interest (SSSIs) and the enforcement of rules governing the use of such land has caused the main problem for wildfowlers. Quite simply all good quality wildfowling land is now encompassed within SSSIs and the NCC has tried to dictate how the sport should be carried out within them; in some cases this has meant no change, but very often sport has had to be substantially curtailed with restrictions including a reduction in actual shooting days on the marsh, limits on the number of Guns per day, bag limits, rest periods and even no-shooting refuges.

The story is complex in the extreme and I do not intend to labour the point further here. Rather I mention the situation as a demonstration of how much our sport has changed over the years. One very real result of NCC interest in SSSI land is that much of this land has been lost to sport forever, via craftily contrived management agreements with land-owners; in too many instances farmers – sadly often shooting men themselves – have sold their souls for a crock of gold, with sport becoming the poorer for this. The end result being more sportsmen chasing less shooting, thereby more restrictions and less actual sporting opportunity for all! All in all the protectionists are doing very well out of the *Wildlife and Countryside Act 1981*. Admittedly, if this *Act* fulfills its prime function of saving further land from going under the plough then us wildfowlers will have benefited substantially – but what a price to pay!

Guns and loads

The *1981 Act* also affected the legal use of our sporting weapons, notably the capacity of semi-automatic and pump-action shotguns. Under the *Act* it became illegal to use either auto or pump against wildfowl or game without the fitment of a plug designed to restrict the magazine to two cartridges; thus the guns became three-shot weapons with the addition of the cartridge in the chamber. Full gun use was still allowed against vermin. Even as this book goes to press the *Firearms (Amendment) Act* nears the statute book, and this will restrict the use of sporting arms still further: now autos and pumps will require PERMANENT modification to ensure the maintenance of the one in the chamber plus two in the magazine format if they are to remain covered by a Shotgun Certificate; unmodified weapons will be subject to full Firearms Certificate controls. As yet it is not known just what parameters are to be issued with regard to such permanent modifications, and it may transpire that it will not be cost-effective to have old guns altered; I suggest that wildfowlers presently using an auto or pump keep a close watch for further news in the sporting press.

The use of automatic, or pump-action, shotguns for wildfowling has long been an emotive subject, with the separate schools of thought prepared to defend their arguments with great vigour. I favour the use of an automatic or pump more because they are cheap and robust weapons than for the extra shot thus allowed when required; if automatics are sometimes prone to jam or some other defect, then the pump is as tough and as oblivious to abuse as any tool one could wish to handle.

At one time I owned an Italian automatic which I used with excellent results for shooting both live and clay pigeons; it was only natural that I should want this high degree of consistency to be present in my wildfowling, instead of being abandoned for a more mediocre standard as soon as I took my magnum out of mothballs. Thus I began to use an automatic for my wildfowling. Another reason for this change was that I had simply out-grown the magnum-orientated way of thinking. After wasting countless pounds on heavy loads over a period of many years I had finally realised that I could kill most of my duck with high velocity game loads – 1⅛ oz of 6 shot. Of course the key to success when using such light loads is to shoot the birds at a comfortable killing range – a premise which should naturally apply to shooting anyway.

Admittedly heavy loads are capable of bringing down some very long range birds, but in all honesty there are few men who are capable of shooting with consistent accuracy at such ranges. The heaviest loads are apt to encourage excessively long range shooting in some cases. Most certainly the younger and less experienced wildfowlers – for advanced age and experience do not necessarily go hand in hand – who seem to be the main users of such loads, are probably less capable of placing their shot on the distant target. Most of the wildfowling done in the saltmarshes, where birds may be coming in to feed, will be carried out in the close to medium range bracket – up to 40 yards. To fire heavy loads of large shot, often from a tightly choked gun, is to place oneself at a considerable disadvantage, for there is no cartridge better suited to this sort of work than a standard load of 6 or 7 shot. Even when armed with light loads it is often surprising just how devastating one's firepower can be; so long as the limitations of the weapon are kept firmly in mind there should be no great problem. To actually hit a close target fair and square with a heavy load may well render it useless for food anyway, thus wasting a valuable and noble quarry. The magnum load has a very special niche on the foreshore: it is for those high flighting birds and for the man who can put his shot squarely on the target. It is a special load for a specialist job.

The correct choice of choke for the job in hand is obviously of equal importance. If a tight choke allows an advantage at long range the opposite will apply at close range, with the following formula about right: long range – larger shot and tight choke; close range – small shot and open choke.

My switch to the automatic and lighter loads came at roughly the same time, and the results were an immediate improvement. I ceased shooting at ultra-long range birds, which saved me many pounds in heavy loads and much disappointment into the bargain, and began to perform much better at those closer chances. My confidence rose accordingly, and as confidence is frequently the harbinger of greater success I was really on the up and up. Sadly, some still think of people who use automatics as trigger-happy cowboys firing terrible barrages at any bird unfortunate to come anywhere near. No doubt there has been a disreputable element which has misused these weapons – although no more so than applies to more traditional double-barrelled guns – but if one has a mind to do so it is possible to abuse anything, whilst there will always be those who are quite willing to give a dog a bad name. Most wildfowlers are thoroughly responsible types, and in such hands the automatic is every bit as respectable as any other type of gun.

There are some who consider it unfair to fire more than two shots at a bird, or pack of birds. A matter of opinion perhaps, but most certainly not one which I subscribe to. I have no hesitation if presented with the opportunity for a third shot, simply remembering all the times that I have come away from the shore without firing a shot. There is a school of thought which decries the use of an automatic for wildfowling, yet accepts the taking of large bags, perhaps 20 or more birds, simply because a double-barrelled gun was being used. Such hypocrisy almost defies description, and demonstrates how muddle-headed some people can be!

Nobody can deny that a gun is only as good as the man behind it and although I use an automatic, or pump, I do so in a proper manner, seldom firing that third shot; yet it is nice to know that I can take full advantage of a chance should it present itself – especially as this may be the only opportunity for several trips. I believe that I deserve this little perk as a reward for all the hard work I put into my sport.

However, like all tools, the little Italian automatic had gradually outlived its usefulness, and has since given way to a cheaper American pump gun whose added bonus is a multichoke capacity – that is a selection of changeable screw-in choke tubes. Now I use improved cylinder for most of my wildfowling, only changing to half or three-quarter choke for those high flighting birds, or when after geese. Additionally the pump gun is also a magnum, thus allowing me to abandon my earlier policy of using the automatic for duck, whilst changing to a heavy over-and-under magnum once the geese arrived. Those two guns were quite dissimilar, with the change frequently causing a spell of inaccurate shooting while I made the adjustment. Now I use the same gun all season long, and shoot inaccurately all the time! (I jest!) The departure of my two old wildfowling guns was almost sad, for they were like old friends, but the change has never been regretted for I find the pump a remarkably suitable weapon.

The small shot theory founders once wild geese are the quarry, for on the exposed shore the magnum load comes into its own. The game load is no match for our most magnificent of aerial quarry; indeed I believe it morally wrong to attempt to tackle such birds with anything less than the heaviest possible load. However, heavy loads need not be synonymous with large pellets, with a 'pattern kills' concept still as relevant as ever. I have now abandoned the use of BB shot altogether as I believe that the pattern is too full of holes by far; even a bird as large as a goose can sometimes owe its life to a bad pattern. Even the giant $1\frac{7}{8}$ oz American loads will throw a pattern full of holes when used at the long range encountered when goose shooting on the shore. Ranges up to 60 yards are not uncommon, so that even a goose can look pretty small at this distance. For me BB shot is a heartbreaker. I admit that the striking power of an individual pellet is fearsome, being capable of snapping the wing bone of a gander with consummate ease, but of all the geese I have shot using BBs none have been hit by more than three pellets. There have been several with broken wings where a single pellet has done the job, whilst several more have glided on when hit in the body.

There can be few more sickening sights than a goose setting those mighty wings into a seemingly endless glide which can easily take the bird beyond reach. There is nothing more soul- destroying in wildfowling than a lost goose – such a terrible waste. One such bird which eluded me by gliding into the gloom of evening flight, was found by a friend the next day where the tide had dumped it on the salting. When plucked it could be seen that two BBs had hit it amidships about three inches apart, and had passed right through the body! This will give some idea of the terrible striking power of BB shot, but will give an even greater insight into the incredible toughness of the wild goose. Of course I shall never know what effect smaller shot might have had; yet it is a fair bet that more pellets from the fuller pattern would have hit that bird, and therefore highly likely that it would have come straight down instead of gliding for half a mile.

For years now I have used American number 2 shot, and have killed more geese as a result of this change. It cannot be emphasised too often that it is the density of the pattern which determines the success of a shot, with so many geese owing longevity to the BB shot that have whistled harmlessly by. Despite the bigger size of the goose it will prove no easier to hit than the smaller ducks. The problems attached to goose shooting are many and diverse, with the many goose shooters throughout the land fully aware of such problems; most such men will be highly experienced and able to hit that elusive quarry with a fair degree of consistency when the opportunity presents itself.

With the exception of punt-gunning, foreshore goose shooting is by far the most demanding form of wildfowling. The return may seem meagre indeed, if one considers the amount of time and effort involved if one is to kill even a single goose. Invariably disappointment will be the result of a foray after the geese, but when success comes it is very sweet indeed. The term 'a wild goose chase' is not some romantic notion from the writer's pen, rather a fitting and apt description of the difficulties attached to the hunting of this wild quarry. As I shall write later in this book, there are few finer ways of spending one's leisure time than in the pursuit of the wild, yodelling skeins.

This chapter has set out the confines within which the modern wildfowler must pursue his sport. The changes have been many, and few of them of benefit to the sport; but, thankfully, we can still hunt wildfowl in something like the traditional manner. Yes, with good fortune I shall still be wildfowling in the year 2008, although I write this in the almost certain knowledge that the option will largely rest in hands other than my own.

—3—

September Days

A FTER THE STRENUOUS events of the opening day have subsided somewhat there is often a curious limbo time on the foreshore. That first early flush of home-bred birds will have been a little dissipated, and unless good fortune prevails most wildfowlers will be hard put to come up with a bird or two. For the beginner this is possibly no bad thing, as it allows him the luxury of getting to know the shore without worrying over much about lost sporting opportunity. Such time will prove to be an investment that may prevent a good deal of heartache and aggravation in the future. I shall elaborate upon this statement a little later on. The more experienced men will react in varying ways. Some will abandon any serious attempt at sport during these balmy September days; others will persevere, knowing full well that this will bring its own rewards eventually; still others might specialise, especially in those areas where certain species predominate – such as Canada geese or golden plover. Of course pre-1982 this period could be taken up by shooting shore waders – a delightfully rewarding occupation in itself.

Two of the major early season problems will be heat, especially ruinous when en route to and from the flighting areas – as I mentioned earlier – and mosquitos. These infuriating insects will be encountered on most foreshore and coastal areas, although they do tend to attack some people more than others. Perhaps to a mosquito I am the equivalent to a good steak dinner. Most certainly they generally bite me with enthusiasm whenever the opportunity arises, the legacy of which will inevitably be red, itching lumps which may take several days to disappear. Now I use one of the excellent repellents on the market, currently favouring a deodorant-type stick which just happens to be highly effective. In some areas the mosquitos are fairly few and far between, tending to attack singly or in small wings. Yet elsewhere they may be present in mighty squadrons of uncountable proportions, hanging as though suspended from some invisible cord in dense clouds. These may appear as puffs of smoke from a distance, but woe betide anyone who ventures near unprotected.

In the gloom of flight mosquitos can be most distracting, for even when smothered in repellent one can scarcely help a quick swat at any insect which may come too close. Such an act invariably occurs at that crucial moment when the only duck of the flight hoves near! Another bane will be the frequent occasions when the insect disguises itself as an approaching duck! So often the brief glimpse of an incoming bird seen from the corner of the eye, and immediately provoking a heart-fluttering response, will materialise into a mosquito hovering at point-blank range! Damn them! Sometimes their attack will be accompanied by a good deal of noise as they dive in, Stuka fashion, whilst equally often there will be a low-level sneak attack. Ignore these warnings at your peril, for quiet or loud the end result will be the same. Ouch!

So where once I sported for shore waders during the limbo time, I am now reduced to grubbing about for the odd bird that might

The partly flooded saltmarsh can be a great draw for duck.

chance my way. Nonetheless this is an easy and relaxing time, and, mosquitos aside, there is little problem attached to flighting.

There are a couple of methods of procuring sport which I favour at this time. One is the flighting of the golden plover and, even though few shots can be had, this is a pleasant enough interlude; the other is to go down to the *zostera* beds in the hope of an odd goldie, mallard, or with great luck an early wigeon. Both methods require the minimum preparation, and attract few real discomforts.

Golden plover flighting

So to the seawall a mile or so from where I knew the goldies were feeding scattered like sparkling beads of shingle on the flat greenery of the grazing marsh. Yes, I knew they would come through, but exactly where and at what height was another matter entirely. If one can predict anything about wildfowl and waders with complete certainty it is that they are totally unpredictable. The warmth of the day died leaving a chill in the air totally typical of the time of year, whilst nothing moved save the semi-hallucinatory mosquito clouds. As always when the goldies came it would be in the last of the light, with slender blurring wings hurtling them forward at often shot-defying speed. Here the light was fairly favourable with the line of flight emanating from the north-west, so that if any flew past to my left they would be silhouetted against the dying embers of the sun where it had splashed red all across the western horizon. If they came to the east they would be mostly invisible against the darkest part of the sky.

The tide was low and silent, and there was precious little wind to mask the sounds of the shore birds going about their business as night drew on. Soon I could hear odd goldies on the wing, the soft fluting whistle presaging the occasional rush of wings, though none came near enough nor flew within my range of vision. Out on the mud the soft contented voices of goldies could be heard from where they had dropped in for a temporary roost, before the surging tide forced them to find drier parts. Once the plaintive wailing voice of the grey plover came from the gathering gloom which masked the flats; such a sad, almost mournful sound this, the call of the grey plover – and so evocative of our southern estuaries. But what did this stout little wader mourn for? How can I tell? Perhaps it mourned the ebbing of the tide, or even the flooding of the tide which would inundate its feeding grounds. Perhaps it mourned the loss of its spectacular summer livery; perhaps the passing of the day, or even that the September night lasts but a few brief hours. Perhaps I imagined the whole thing!

As so often occurs they came with a scything rush of wings, so that I barely had time to react before a party of four swept past like tiny bullets. Just time to stand upright and fire a single shot, and I was a little surprised to see a bird fall. Three more shots at them as they hurtled past produced another single bird – not a bad average at fast sporting birds in such bad light. I laid them gently in the springy grasses on the seawall. They were a riot of speckled gold, their slender bodies remarkably unsullied by the shots that had lain them to rest; no blood, and barely a feather out of place. The loss of these fine sporting birds was nothing in the context of life on the estuary, for their place had been a minute one in the great order of things. There were a thousand, and yet more thousands, to take their place; truly the effect of the wildfowlers' activities are minimal, which is something those opposed to our sport would do well to consider.

A pair of snipe went rasping their way inland, in search of some soft feeding place. At my insistent calling they turned and crossed the seawall to my west at a comfortable range; but they were much slower than the hair-brained goldies, and I missed them completely. I waited on as the west turned black in the vain hope that a teal or mallard might put in an appearance. But only the angry presence of the mosquito squadrons, denied a meal by the repellent which protected me, disturbed the tranquil scene. Though I detest these pests I suppose that the mosquito has as much right to its niche on the coast as does the golden plover; perhaps without such ugliness we should fail to appreciate the beauty of such as the goldie, and thereby be all the poorer as a result.

Thus the end of another flight – an easy, relaxed sojourn at the base of a stone-clad earthen seawall. Wildfowling at its least demanding with scarcely any need to dress up in full 'uniform', although the mosquitos will discourage excessive nudity. Then a silent trudge back to the waiting car, with two dead goldies for company, and the grudging twinkling light from the myriad stars in that inky void above.

The next day I tried another area, some miles away. Here I knew there might be a few goldies, with just the chance of a shot at a mallard. I had done well there in the past, and always found a sense of optimism pervaded whenever I skulked in this salting close to the seawall. An early start was always to be advised, so that the tide had scarcely turned in late afternoon when I arrived to take up station in the tall sea aster close to the tide's edge. This was taking the sport a little further, without actually becoming heavily involved in venturing across the open muds or into the creek-cut tangle of saltmarsh. No danger and precious little inconvenience. The necessity of wearing full weatherproof gear at all times when on the shore was emphasised on this day, for it came on to rain. Firstly in light desultory fashion, but progressively harder as the day began to fade, until it was positively throwing it down sufficiently to soak the dog, gun and all my gear – although I remained relatively dry within my snug cocoon.

As ever the first scouting parties of waders appeared to search for any exposed feeding site. This will occur even before the first of the mud is uncovered and the sense of timing of these little birds is one of the marvels of the coast; for they know that the tide should soon be away, and become impatient to set themselves down in its margins at the first opportunity. Just a small flight of redshank, or solitary dunlin skimming the salting edge until they find a safe feeding place; once these first birds are down, the rest will follow soon enough, until the whole shore is a-twitter with feeding birds. At this time one can easily lapse into a reverie of watching the waders come down with the ebb of the tide, and to do so is to provoke the inevitable wasted chance at some quarry bird or other. So it proved on this day, for as I watched the antics of some feeding redshank, three snipe (cunningly impersonating wave-hopping dunlin) came on to me before I woke up and identified them. I fired belatedly, but knocked one down into the shallow water, from where the dog retrieved it with great gusto and much splashing and snorting.

At length, with the tide ebbing rapidly, the rain left off and a little more colour began to return to the drenched saltmarsh. Nonetheless, the sky was still grey and somber-looking, and with night now approaching rapidly the eastern sky looked very gloomy and foreboding. A pair of teal swept the outer edge of the salting, totally ignoring my seductive calling, and landed upon a newly exposed piece of mud. They stood rigidly alert, suspiciously stretching their short necks as they studied their surroundings prior to getting down to the serious business of dibbling in the slush left behind by the tide. The binoculars showed me their every detail, before they eventually took off to search for alternative feeding elsewhere on the coast. A few goldies burst past, aided and abetted by a breeze that had begun to spring from the west. After six shots without touching a feather I realised that they were much too quick for me; thereafter, I gave the next bird a huge lead, in excess of eight feet, and killed it stone dead. Having got the measure of them it was fairly predictable that no more should appear.

No doubt as a result of the freshening breeze, the clouds off to the west began to break up and slowly the setting sun slid down from behind the dark canopy. For a few moments it became a fiery ball of red and orange, to light up the whole horizon to its north and south in a great slash of blazing red, a slash which spread with great speed amongst the broken clouds until the entire western sky seemed alight. Slowly, almost imperceptibly, the sun slid down towards the horizon. Slowly it slid out of sight behind the nearby hill, so that the small cluster of buildings standing there were etched against the sky: the chimney pots of the houses; the uprights of the telephone poles; the gaunt structure of a barn and the pointed spire of a little-used church. Soon the sun had disappeared, but the redness lingered on long after the departure of its maker. How can one value a sunset such as this? Truly the wildfowler, perhaps more than any other, will see such incredible sights throughout his long 'career'; but though they may become less of a rarity, such beauties will never be commonplace, for on each occasion there will be that same breath-catching excitement. Such an experience is beyond price, and is just one of the many reasons why we love our time on the foreshore so much.

Against the last dregs of the light I saw three mallard some way off inland. They responded to my calling instantly, passing me at a nice 40 yards or so, even if they were a little difficult to pick out in the bad light; as they passed I fired a single shot, for one bird to fall into the mud with a loud smack. A fitting finalé to a wonderfully stimulating afternoon. As I began the long walk back the rain began to fall again, softly with an almost mistlike quality. It was a time to reflect on the events of the afternoon on the edge of the saltmarsh: how unchanged everything appeared, as though time had stood still since my last visit to that area during the previous season; indeed in many ways this is true, for the shore changes but little, whilst the changes that do occur are mostly slight and imperceptible, unless Man rudely lends a hand to tarnish the work of Nature.

The zostera beds
So, as September draws on, and hop-gathering time is upon this fair county of Kent, I make my way to the *zostera* beds, more by way of finding peace and solitude than with any realistic hope of bagging a duck. Few wildfowlers frequent this place, for it is mostly

unproductive in terms of birds in the bag; nevertheless there is much to savour, whilst for the tyro there exists abundant opportunity for learning another aspect of the sport. The flats are of course only tenable at low water, with the tide receding into the deep and mostly only visible as a grey scar in the middle distance. These flats drain with astonishing rapidity once the ebb begins in earnest, although conversely tending to flood with rather disarming speed; this is one of the reasons why such places can prove deathtraps for the unwary when conditions are less than favourable – especially where darkness and fog may combine to confuse the wildfowler.

This place seems friendly and innocuous enough under the warming rays of an autumn afternoon sun, nor are there any creeks which can flood early and thereby trap you on the open flats. But one can scarcely afford to treat the shore or the tide with such scant regard if your desire is to become an old and wise sportsman. Here too the mud is mostly firm and good to walk upon, but not all flats will be the same. Other parts of the country have similar flats where there are quicksands and soft patches, and creeks which quickly fill with freezing water once the tide begins to flood. Local knowledge, astutely and diligently gained, is vital if the wildfowler is to avoid coming to grief.

Of all the wildfowlers' aids the compass is perhaps the most vital. It will take up little room, and will probably remain unused all

Hard going in the muddy estuary.

season long, but one day it may just save your life. Take a bearing from your flighting place back to safety – for even the magic of a compass will be useless unless you know where the seawall lies! – and remember it against the time when fog may come down so dense as to blot out everything; at such a time even the best of wildfowlers can become totally disorientated, and there is no shame in taking a few sensible precautions. If there are creeks, learn when they will flood, and make sure that you leave sufficient time to beat a safe retreat. Tidal movements are rife with variables and I shall discuss this in greater depth later when we consider shooting on saltmarshes.

Here one can only find real solitude once the light has begun to fade, for these flats play host to many millions of lugworms – a favourite bait with sea anglers. All through the low tide period the bait-diggers can be seen at work, with the disruptive effect on feeding or roosting birds obviously considerable; this is one activity which is quite incompatible with the prolific growth of *zostera*, as this species of marine grass needs a stable stratum in which to grow and does not take kindly to being continually uprooted. Far out across the flats lie great swathes of mussel beds and here too are standing pools left behind by the tide; it is a useful place to lie in ambush for duck, whilst the pools are ideal for depositing a few decoys which, together with skilful calling, can often make the difference between being successful and otherwise. Similarly shallow pools exist on the *zostera* itself, and here too decoys can sometimes work.

A handy pool for decoying on the open flats.

43

There is absolutely no cover on the flats, and it will be necessary to wear full wildfowling regalia as protection against the effects of adopting a prone position at flight time. This is as uncomfortable and messy a shooting method as one could hope to find, and scarcely conducive to accurate shooting either, however the only alternative is to dig a hole which will prove equally messy and very hard work into the bargain. Duck will soon spot any object obviously out of place on the shore, and will mostly give it a wide berth, so adopt that prone position if you wish to get a shot or two. To ease the inevitable neck-ache it is wise to prop the head on some low 'pillow' – I often use my binocular case for this – and in this way it will be easier to see approaching birds. Similarly if the feet can be on a slightly lower level to the backside this will make the business of sitting up to shoot that much easier. Lie facing the expected line of flight, or the decoy pattern. In this way it will be easier to sit up and swing to the right or left as the birds veer away. This type of shooting can never be described as easy, but is a method well worth cultivating and is a valuable addition to the wildfowlers' repertoire of skills.

Windy days should be avoided as the birds seem to favour the cold windswept flats rather less. Far better to choose quieter evenings when the duck will swing round and round searching for a suitable feeding place; under such conditions the birds are more likely to see the decoys and respond to the call.

As always I waited for the light to begin to fade before walking out. A huge stand of several hundred goldies departed with much piping at my approach, for the area is often a favourite secondary roost, whilst a pair of mallard left the mussels and sped off in the direction of the main channel. Par for the course really. The *zostera* was in good order, although I knew that very soon the first of the Brent geese would be arriving to graze here, and once the main flocks arrived the tasty marine grass would quickly be eaten out. Until then a few wigeon might get a feed, and with luck I might get a chance or two at them.

It took only a few moments to deposit a dozen decoys, strung together and weighted, into adjacent pools and to settle down on an old sheet of plastic brought for the purpose. The plastic would allow me to avoid the worst of the mud and water, and thereby encourage swift and decisive action should the opportunity arise. There just remained the task of settling the dog beside me, clasping the gun lightly across my stomach, and awaiting events. This is a peaceful time on the open shore and the impression of timelessness is heightened. One is left to reflect that this shore must have been this way, largely unchanged, for centuries, and would continue this way on into infinity in all probability.

A few goldies rushed past as the light drew in. They were very quick, and I paid them no heed at such a late hour for I did not want to alarm any duck that might be abroad. One has always had to temper wader shooting enthusiasm with realism in case bigger fare happened to be about. The slightest of chills began to settle over me. October lay just around the corner, and a few weeks hence the frosts would begin, and the downward spiral into deep winter would begin in earnest. Soon the migratory ducks and geese upon which we wildfowlers rely for the bulk of our sport would begin arriving en mass, filling our estuaries with noisy colourful multitudes of birds fit to drive a fellow half crazy. A wonderfully exciting time lay ahead, and such thoughts made the more mundane times of early season all the more tolerable.

The sun, now departed, had touched the west with gold, which now glistened back off the mud in a wash of shining light, against which the occasional tiny wader could be seen probing energetically for food. Soon even that light would be gone, whilst already the stars were out; not a sound of duck wings or voices anywhere, and a blank seemed an almost certainty.

Then the barest glimpse of duck silhouettes in the west before they were gone again – four maybe five birds. I let out a succession of hopeful calls at intervals, held the gun even tighter, and prepared myself lest the hurtling black shapes come out of the

gloom with scarcely any warning. The seconds dragged slowly by, but nothing else occurred. Then far away across the darkened flats came a melodic, yet piercing whistle, then again a trifle closer this time so that the hackles on my neck gave a little flutter as the poignancy of the moment had its effect. I had not heard that sound since February, and now the first of the wigeon packs were back. That whistle told a story almost, for it came like a slice of the wilderness of the far-off tundra; it told of the desperate southerly flight in front of the advancing winter storms, and of the final joyful landing in a warm and mostly hospitable land.

The wigeon were back and the wild, whistling packs would be there to challenge the wildfowler from this day to the season's close. Sometimes we would succeed in getting on terms with them, but mostly they would win through, so that the vast flocks would once again be winging their way northward with the nearing of the spring.

—4—

The Shore and the Quarry

ALREADY I HAVE MENTIONED the use of binoculars on more than one occasion, and with good reason too. For the dedicated wildfowler his binoculars are almost as much a part of his equipment as is his gun. This is no casual exaggeration either, for whether used for vital reconnaissance work or more casual ornithology, the binoculars go to make the day that much more enjoyable.

As will be seen throughout these pages, the wildfowler spends a vast proportion of his time on the shore just sitting and watching all that goes on around him. He will be ensconced in some secretive hideaway in the saltmarsh from where he will see without being seen, and will learn much about his surroundings as a result; it is no coincidence that so many experienced wildfowlers are also good naturalists and ornithologists, for if they were not blessed with such proficiency they could hardly expect to succeed at their sport. Most facets of life are a question of give and take: the more time and effort that you are prepared to invest, then mostly the rewards will be that much greater. And wildfowling is no great exception – unless you put yourself out you can scarcely expect a consistently good return. This is really the hallmark of a good wildfowler – consistency; he is the man who will keep coming back with something in the bag, even when conditions are basically unfavourable.

In many ways the dedicated wildfowler and the dedicated ornithologist have a great deal in common, far more than some would readily admit. Some of the finest ornithologists in the land are, or have been, wildfowlers and basically their aims are the same: both want to get as close to the birds as they can, are fascinated by both bird and its vital sustaining habitat, and want for nothing

Using binoculars to keep an eye on duck movement.

more than to see the overall well-being of each species. In addition
the wildfowler expects to cull what is after all a harvestable surplus,
but this is the only thing which separates the two groups of
enthusiasts. The wildfowler probably comes to more intimate
terms with the shore birds than the great majority of ornithologists,
for he sees these birds at those most secret of times when darkness
spreads across the land and all good folk are safe indoors. He sees
the birds as they come to the shore in a joyful rush of pinions; he
hears them talk, in gentle secretive tones, as they busy themselves
amongst the slushes in search of some vital sustaining food. Yes, it
is a soft and secret time, and belongs to the birds and the wildfowler
that hunts them in the time-honoured manner.

The experienced, dedicated ornithologists are perhaps less
plentiful than one would like, although their number is growing all
the time. They will take a leaf out of the wildfowler's book and see
without being seen wherever possible; many of these men
understand the case for wildfowling, and realise that responsible
wildfowlers do untold good for the well-being of our estuary birds.
The two pastimes are really quite compatible. Yet much ill-feeling
exists between the two camps, much of which will be generated by
the attitude of so many of those who just want to watch. Of course,
it would be churlish to try and suggest that the blame for any
ill-feeling is all one-sided, for there are some wildfowlers who do
their cause no good at all by their thoughtless behaviour.

One swallow does not a summer make. By the same token, it takes a great deal more than a gun to make a wildfowler, and more than a pair of binoculars to make an ornithologist. A number of years ago wildfowling was dogged by the reprehensible behaviour of what were then termed 'marsh cowboys'; thankfully today the species is largely extinct, due largely to stricter control of coastal areas by landowners and wildfowling clubs. I suggest that the behaviour of many who aspire to ornithology is on a par with the 'marsh cowboy'. They can scarcely merit the prestigious title of ornithologist, so better to call them birdwatchers and leave it at that. They know precious little of what occurs on the coast – in short they see without seeing. Their behaviour is often appalling for they wander where they will, having little regard for Reserve boundaries or for the real needs of the birds they purport to protect; misguidedly they think that because they do no actual physical harm they are harmless. They seldom pause to think, for example, where 10,000 waders disturbed from their high tide roost will finish up.

If wildfowling be governed to a large extent by the weather, then so too should ornithology. For the conditions which enable the wildfowler to come to terms with his quarry must also be a bonus to the dedicated watcher of birds. But how often does one encounter the ornithologist crouching in the saltings waiting for the teal to flight in at dusk, or skulking beside some inland fleet waiting for the mallard or wigeon to come once the stars are twinkling

Sheltered creeks and bays are an attraction to duck when the estuary is rough.

overhead? Can they be found waiting in the moonlight for the wigeon to flight to the floods or the *zostera* beds, or waiting for the geese to flight at dawn? Quite simply they miss so many of the things that are worth seeing.

Of course, ornithologists possessing this level of dedication do exist, but they are few and far between. Those who have read the works of that brilliant naturalist Richard Perry may be familiar with his book *At the Turn of the Tide*. In it he describes many things that normally only the wildfowler sees, he expresses feelings that I often thought unique to the wildfowler, and, if one did not know better, one could be forgiven for thinking that Perry is a wildfowler. But he is not – he is an ornithologist of the highest order. He brings a flair and a dedication to ornithology that is sorely needed; no doubt his solitary vigils in the freezing cold and darkness were rewarded in a suitable manner, and I wish him well. His knowledge is awe-inspiring, his methods and attitude commendable – I wish there were more like him.

In the days, long since past, when it was possible to earn a living, albeit ever so frugal, from wildfowling, these professionals must have possessed enormous knowledge, for without this knowledge they would have most certainly starved. There could have been very little that they did not know about their coastal environment, although their attitude was of course mercenary, and in complete contrast to the attitudes of modern-day enthusiasts. It is this professional approach which will yield the greatest reward, for if we imagine that we shall starve without a vast knowledge of what occurs on the shore, then we will learn all the quicker. In these modern times, shorn of the need to make a living from our quarry, we are better placed to enjoy our surroundings – it is an opportunity which should not be frittered away.

Understanding the shore
So where do we begin if we wish for a fuller understanding of the shore? Well, perhaps first of all we must all appreciate that wild birds do nothing by chance; outside of the breeding season their only interest is to find sufficient food for their needs, and some safe roosting site to while away the hours not spent on the feeding grounds. If the birds are on the shore at a given time they are there for a very good reason. Find out what this reason is and you are well on the way to understanding the birds, and thereafter en route to putting something in the bag. Easy, isn't it?!

If we are to consider the quarry, and be able to identify each species before it is put in the bag, we must first look at the shore and the movements of the birds. Whilst at times certain species will be feeding on the shore, they will invariably be off somewhere inland taking advantage of richer pickings; the story of the season is very much about a breakdown into periods when certain conditions prevail, and thereby certain foodstuffs will become readily available to the hungry flocks. In general terms wild duck will feed during the hours of darkness, before retiring to some safe roost during the daylight hours; geese are the opposite, feeding during the daylight hours before returning to their roost at dusk. There are countless variables when the birds will behave in some other way, and I shall deal with some of them from time to time; suffice to say that wildfowl are fickle in the extreme, and this is one of the reasons that the sport tends to be such a complexity when studied in any depth.

Most roosts will be on open mud flats or shallow inshore waters, with birds flighting to feed either inland or on the saltmarsh itself, and very often such movements will occur within a fairly well defined area, or flightline. Although in many instances the birds will be flying too high to present the sportsman with any worthwhile opportunity, given favourable conditions, i.e. a strong headwind, it will be possible to enjoy some sport. This really forms the basis of most wildfowling – ambushing wildfowl on the flightlines. Alternatively birds may be ambushed as they come to

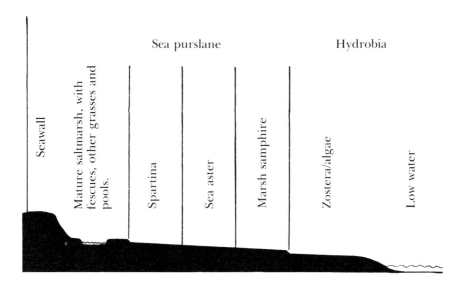

Cross section of the shore.

51

Eel grass (Zostera).

Sea aster (Aster tripolium).

Hydrobia.

Dense growths of algae (typically Enteromorpha *and* Ulva lactuca).

*Marsh samphire (*Salicornia).

*Cord grass (*Spartina).

*Sea purslane (*Halimione portulacoides).

the shore to feed, which they will do spasmodically throughout the season – dependant on the availability of food – but sometimes in considerable numbers. Shooting birds on the roosts is a practice generally frowned upon, and quite rightly so as this is a certain way of persuading birds to leave an area completely; however, under certain circumstances, such as when birds are using some secondary roost, often the more sheltered creeks at high tide during stormy weather, then this is a legitimate and ethical means of sporting for wildfowl.

The typical estuary will provide a veritable banquet for both wildfowl and waders, for such areas are incredibly fertile and will support an abundance of food in the form of invertebrates, molluscs, plants and algae. Where full plant succession occurs there will be a wide variety of food, all of which will prove attractive from time to time. The lower shore, or flats, may support *zostera* grass and such algae as *enteromorpha*, and these will prove valuable to such as the wigeon, a grazing duck, and the non-quarry brent goose. However, *enteromorpha*, with its very high water content, is mostly taken in times of hard weather, and is certainly less valued as food. The lower reaches of the saltmarsh will support the succulent tubular *salicornia*, or marsh samphire; this often occurs in dense beds, and will be much valued by species such as teal and pintail. In many places these open flats and *salicornia* beds, and also the many creeks which dissect most substantial saltmarshes, will be festooned with the tiny snail, *hydrobia*; this is a valued food for many species of duck and forms the bulk of the diet of that handsome non-quarry bird the shelduck.

As the wildfowler moves back from the *salicornia* beds towards the seawall he will find the middle zone of the saltmarsh where both *spartina* and sea aster predominate; often this part of the salting will be particularly dense, and provide less food than can be found on the lower levels. However, in October much seed will fall from these two plant species, and this high-protein food will join the *hydrobia* on the salting floor. Many ducks, including mallard, will take advantage of a bonanza which may last several weeks. On the creek edges grows the shrubby sea purslane. This is seldom sought after as food, but in times of hard weather the wigeon may be obliged to graze upon its thick fleshy leaves; at such a time it may well prove a life saver, with great flocks sometimes seen on the saltings. Finally on the high, mature saltmarsh, close by the seawall, the wildfowler will find the true marsh grasses such as sea meadow grass and fescues, and often such areas will be dotted with pools of standing water with the grasses being grazed by cattle.

Where the grass is short and sweet, and with water close by, wigeon will often come to graze. Some saltmarshes, notably around the Wash and further north, can boast superb wigeon flighting at those times when they are feeding on this rich green sward. If the wildfowler does his homework well he will have learnt all this, and thereby increased manifold the likelihood of adding a bird or two to the bag. For the tyro the problem of identification can be a considerable one, so that any aid will be sought after and valued. To find the experienced wildfowler identifying birds from afar unaided by binoculars often appears little short of miraculous, but it is the result of a practised eye and much more besides.

Short grass next to a salting pool.

IDENTIFICATION

A certain amount of identification can be achieved by association. That is certain species are more likely to be found in an area which fulfills their needs; here local knowledge and a little forethought will help. A breakdown of the nine quarry species of duck will illustrate the point well enough. Of the nine, two are diving ducks – tufted and common pochard – which means that they will swim considerable distances underwater in order to feed; one – the goldeneye – is a marine diving duck, which feeds by diving in estuarine waters; whilst the other six are all dabbling ducks, which feed by dibbling in slushy margins or by upending in shallow water. Of these dabblers, two have rather specialist diets; the wigeon is a grazing duck; whilst the shoveler feeds on tiny morsels sieved through its strange shovel-like bill. The mallard is highly ubiquitous and will take anything from grain to insects, and it is for this reason that it is by far the most numerous duck in the Northern Hemisphere. The teal, pintail and gadwall will all take a variety of seed and small molluscs and are all well adapted to life on the estuary.

It may seem curious to any casual observer that our wetlands can support such huge numbers of so many different species. There is a simple enough explanation for this – comparatively few actually compete for the same food. Really this is as fine an example of natural selection at work as one could wish to find, with, in most cases, the shape of a bird's bill providing the vital clue to its lifestyle. The photographs of heads will demonstrate this far more graphically than words. The four ducks demonstrate bills designed

Wigeon.

Shelduck.

Mallard.

Curlew.

Teal.

Avocet.

for a particular job: thus the wigeon has that small neat, goose-like bill which reliably informs the observer that this is the tool of a grazing bird; the teal has a flatter, broader bill which indicates a preference for seed and small molluscs; the mallard has a less delicate bill which is really in keeping with its wide-ranging diet, whilst the shelduck possesses an almost comical Donald Duck-like upturned bill which is superbly adapted for sieving such as *hydrobia* from the estuarine mud.

Waders provide the most obvious example of natural selection, with the short bill of the plover differing totally from the long snipe bill. With shore waders Nature also varies the length of the legs, so that a multiplicity of leg length and bill length and shape demonstrates how great hosts can feed side by side and yet all find sufficient for their needs. As I mentioned earlier, life on the shore can be very complex when you start to look closely. The photographs of bird heads shows two exaggerated examples of this in the curlew and avocet. Both have huge curving bills, adapted for either deep probing or crafty sieving; other bill shapes pale into insignificance in comparison, although all will prove equally effective.

The identification photographs in this book are all taken from museum specimens, and this has been done with good reason. Reference to these will ensure that there is no possible room for error when confronted by wild birds in the static situation, with variations in gender also being well illustrated. Of course such pictures will be of less value when the wildfowler is confronted by will-o-wisp birds at the gloomy time of flight, but under such circumstances no single set of photographs or drawings can do full justice to the task set them. The illustrations have been arranged in an order which places families of birds together; such families have basic similarities – invariably indicated by the latin prefix – and although the list of inclusions is by no means exhaustive it does cover most of those species most commonly found in the U.K. One or two of these groupings in fact contain birds which are not directly related, but have an associated interest such as habitat usage.

The purchase of a good Field Guide is an absolute essential first step, and I recommend that the emergent wildfowler buys one at an early stage in his career. This used in association with these photographs and notes, and of course observations made in the field, will ensure that the wildfowler ultimately becomes a competent ornithologist – as indeed he must if he is to pursue his sport with distinction.

THE BLACK GEESE

The black geese (*Branta*) are represented by three photographs, although there are principally four species present in the U.K. each winter. The common characteristic is the black legs, feet and bill, whilst plumages will invariably be a contrasting mix of black, white and greys.

Canada geese

*Canada (*Branta canadensis*)*.

The Canada is the only quarry goose amongst these four, and is by far the largest, with adult birds frequently in the 15+ lb bracket. Originally imported from North America for cosmetic purposes, this bird is less' of a wildfowler's goose than any other; it is essentially urban-based, frequenting parks and gardens in great raucous flocks, and thus providing less sport than overall numbers might suggest. It is quite unmistakable in flight, being mostly a low flying giant, very vocal with a deep resonant call as a fitting compliment to its vast size.

Barnacle geese

Barnacle (Branta leucopsis). *Protected*

A glance at the barnacle reveals similarities to the Canada, although any resemblance is largely superficial. This goose is far smaller, being nearer in size to the mallard with short, fast beating wings and a love for flying in great untidy, noisily yapping flocks. Regional association is useful with the barnacle, as it is found mostly on the Western Isles and the west coast of Scotland. The heavily contrasting upper plumage of grey, black and white, together with the white face are unmistakable methods of identification.

Brent geese

Brent (Branta branta bernicla). *Protected*

The brent illustrated is the Russian dark-bellied and again regional/habitat association are invaluable for it is almost exclusively confined to the east and south coast estuaries and the immediate hinterland. This species is also a small, quick-winged goose, with a distinct bias towards an estuarine diet; its throaty 'brup' becomes a distinctive buzz when the birds flock, which they do in untidy swarms often numbering hundreds of birds. Despite the paler underbelly this bird gives a distinct all black impression, whilst the white half-moon above the tail – which is common to all the geese described – serves to heighten this impression. The light-bellied brent (*B.b.hrota*) has a much paler underbelly than its cousin, but otherwise regional association will prove fairly reliable. Its wintering strongholds are in Ireland, and on the west coast, with little overlap between the two species.

THE GREY GEESE

The grey geese (*Anser*) represent what the lay person generally knows and understands as geese: they are highly vocal, alert at all times, and famous for their neat and orderly lines and skeins when in flight – skeins which can often number hundreds of birds. These are principally represented by three common species in the U.K., although there are various sub-species some of which I shall mention. Four species are illustrated, with perhaps the greylag most widely known. Variations of this species occur, although for greatest ease I shall mention only two.

The greylag

Greylag (Anser anser).

The greylag is the forerunner of our huge grey domestic geese and, as the photograph shows, has that same heavily-built frame and stout head and neck. Adult birds bear speckled black on the underbelly, but the most certain identification is the pale grey forewing which is quite outstanding. All grey geese may be reliably identified by voice, and by unique bill, feet and leg colourations. Thus the voice of the greylag is the typical deep nasal crank of the farmyard goose; the bill will be either orange (or pink in *A.a.rubrirostris*) while the feet and legs are pink. Greylag may be found throughout the U.K. in winter.

Pinkfoot geese

*Pinkfoot (*Anser brachyrhynchus*).*

There is no chance of confusion with the smaller, slighter pinkfoot – despite the common pink feet and legs. The pinkfoot has a distinctive, slender black and pink bill, a darker head and neck, and crucially a higher pitched 'wink-wink' call. Pinkfeet may be found from The Wash northwards, with the main flocks in Scotland. The pinkfoot and greylag represent the mainstay of quarry geese in this country, with total numbers well in excess of 200,000 birds.

Bean goose

Bean (Anser fabalis). *Protected*

In contrast the closely related bean goose is an uncommon visitor, and probably justifies its protected status. Legs are orange, with the bill black and orange; it too sports a dark head and neck, although the call is deeper pitched and less exciting than that of the pinkfoot.

The European white-front
The final photograph shows the remaining quarry goose – the European white-front. Its range is confined almost exclusively to the southern part of the country where it can occur in congregations numbering several thousands. The adult is arguably the most handsome of our grey geese, with the grey plumage being highlighted by the pure white forehead and heavily black-barred chest; legs and feet are orange whilst the bill is pink. Many wildfowling authors have called this the 'laughing goose', as a tribute to its very high-pitched, almost hysterical call. The immature bird lacks both white forehead and black bars. The white-front is a protected bird in Scotland, which is mainly because any birds which occur are likely to belong to the much scarcer Greenland race (*A.a.flavirostris*), whose main wintering range is Ireland and the Western Isles. The species is similar to its European cousin, yet sports a darker head and neck and an

European white-front (Anser anser albifrons).

orange-yellow bill. In flight the white-front has noticeably narrower wings than other grey geese, and this can sometimes aid identification where a flock stays silent. A vagrant which may sometimes occur is the lesser white-front (*A. erythropus*). The bird is slightly smaller than the other white-fronts, has an extended white forehead and a yellow ring around the eye.

SHELDUCK

Shelduck (Tadorna tadorna). *Protected*

The only shelduck with which I shall deal is the commonly seen species (*Tadorna tadorna*). This large handsome duck is the denizen of the open estuary mudflats and oozes where it guzzles *hydrobia* and other prey. The photograph shows its contrasting plumage, which is black, white and chestnut, and this species is totally dissimilar to any other likely to be encountered. For positive identification in bad light the near white plumage and the slow measured wingbeat, from which a loud whispering emanates, will distinguish it from the similar sized mallard. The call is a loud laughing quacking in the female, and a pleasing soft whistle in the drake.

DABBLING DUCK

Wings of dabblers: clockwise mallard, wigeon and shoveler.

As stated earlier in the text six of our quarry duck are dabblers, and the photographs also include the protected summer migrant garganey. So the family *Anas* all have basic similarities: they jump cleanly from land or water; walk, swim and dive adequately, and fly swiftly and in some cases almost acrobatically. The photographs demonstrate the differences in build and plumage, although further elaboration will be needed to aid identification in the field.

If grey geese have unique bill and leg colouration as a reliable means of identification, then the *Anas* have uniquely coloured wing patches – speculum. The photograph shows three species with markedly different speculum, whilst with some species, such as the cock wigeon, there are other characteristics; in good light some speculum can be very noticeable, but can generally only be relied upon for identification at close quarters.

So how does the experienced wildfowler identify distant flighting duck with such apparent ease and confidence? Largely through experience gained over a period of years, but also via a number of clues such as flight, congregation, habitat association and the most reliable method of all – sound. The most common species present few problems for even the relatively inexperienced.

The mallard

Mallard (Anas platyrhynchos).

The mallard is the largest of the dabblers, and is really unmistakable with its broad wings, long neck and distinctive sizzling wingbeat; often seen in large packs, flying in tidy formation, during the early part of the winter it will mostly be found in pairs or small parties, and can be found anywhere near or on the coast. The speculum is blue, edged with white. The duck is highly vocal, being responsible for the strident 'quack, quack, quack' so often heard wherever there is water; in flight a joyful low stuttering quack may be heard, while the much quieter drake offers a soft sibilant 'kneap'.

The teal

*Teal (*Anas crecca).

Almost as well known is the teal, and again instantly recognisable by its small size and rapid dashing flight. Found throughout our coastal areas it is known for its tight-packed formations and incredibly rapid flight; there is no audible wingbeat, rather a tearing sound as air passes over rapidly beating pinions. Teal may be found singly or in packs containing scores of birds. The cock has a delightful fluted whistle, whilst the hen issues either a harsh 'quack' or a short nasal 'kneap'. The speculum is green and black with a white or buff leading edge.

The garganey
The protected garganey is seldom present after the first few weeks of the season, for it soon migrates south to warmer climes. Very similar to the teal, chief identifying characteristics will be the paler wings and back, with a paler more contrasting belly; it is seldom seen in large packs, being far less gregarious than the teal. The green speculum lacks any black and is edged with white. The cock emits a low grating sound, and the hen a low 'quack'. A difficult identification problem in bad light with the slightly larger size not to be relied upon to distinguish this species from the teal, and we may be pleased that it is not an over-wintering species.

Garganey (Anas querquedula). *Protected*

The wigeon

Wigeon (Anas penelope).

The wigeon is our other very well-known dabbler, and can scarcely be confused with other species. Fast flying, although scarcely so swift as the teal, it can produce an audible swift wingbeat, but equally often produces a great sighing of air as flocks stream overhead. More often than not the wigeon will appear in great packs and is generally kind to anyone seeking to learn wildfowl identification. Curving sickle-shaped wings and white belly are reliable aids; the greenish speculum is not that striking, but in the adult cock the spectacular white shoulder is easily noticeable in low flying birds. The voice is one of the best known and most evocative of all wildfowl – the cock emitting a wild, far-carrying whistle, with the hen a soft throaty growl; the commotion made by massed packs of flighting birds has to be heard to be believed.

The Pintail

Pintail (Anas acuta).

Pintail are nationally far less common, but are locally abundant in certain favoured estuaries. A large duck, near the size of the mallard, it is a steady and stately flyer with long wings and long drawn out profile occasioned by the long neck and tail. The drake has long pin feathers – from whence the name was derived – with its long neck being the main distinguishing feature; in the drake the head may appear divorced from the body, an illusion created by the whiteness of most of the neck. Often seen in pairs or small packs, with a whispering audible wingbeat. The drake has a low-pitched whistle and the duck emits a low growl, although this is generally a fairly quiet species. Speculum is black tinged bronze-green, with a yellowish leading edge.

The shoveler

Shoveler (Anas clypeata).

The shoveler is another species which is seen in favoured localities, and greatly prefers a freshmarsh environment to the adjacent saltings. The drake is a riot of colour, with the white chest being visible at some distance; chief identifying characteristics are the rapid flight, creating a teal-like wing-tearing sound, a fairly small size and an ungainly front-heavy appearance due to that huge spatula bill. The speculum is green with a white leading edge, whilst the pale blue shoulder is a notable feature in good light. One of the quieter species, the shoveler cannot be relied upon in winter to offer any worthwhile clue as to identity via the voice.

The gadwall

The final photograph depicts the gadwall, a medium-sized duck which also prefers the fresh marsh. Smaller than the mallard it nonetheless shares many mallard traits such as diet and habitat; it has a mallard-like wingbeat, although a trifle faster, and may generally be seen in small packs. The pale belly is a good clue as to

*Gadwall (*Anas strepera*).*

identity, whilst in good light the white speculum is the best aid of all. The voice of the drake is a low, almost comical croak, with the duck emitting a quiet 'quack'.

DIVING DUCK

Diving duck are represented by four photographs, with two being freshwater duck and two essentially marine-based. Diving duck characteristically run across the surface of the water with furiously beating wings in order to take off, but once airborne have a rapid flight which usually makes a swift rattling sound which can be heard for some distance. There is no reliable speculum.

The common pochard

The common pochard is a bird of freshwater pools and brackish fleets and ditches where it dives for vegetation. Seldom encountered on the shore it can nonetheless be locally common and may be ambushed by flighting tactics; quite often the pochard can be seen in large packs, flying in an orderly formation. Its colouring is fairly uniform below, and this usually serves to distinguish it from the other, lighter-coloured, diving duck; the species is fairly silent, with the drake having a sharp whistle and the duck a hoarse growl.

Common Pochard (Aythya ferina).

The tufted duck

Tufted (Aythya fuligula).

The tufted shares much pochard habitat, but dives for molluscs in the main. Somewhat smaller than the pochard, the sharply contrasting white belly is a reliable means of identification; the drake emits a pleasant whistle whilst the duck has the typical diving duck growl. Both sexes have a white wing bar.

The scaup

Scaup (Aythya marila). *Protected*

As the photographs show, the marine scaup is very similar to the tufted, although a little larger; with this species habitat association is a valuable method of helping with identification as it is seldom found close inshore except in time of hard weather. As it is so similar to the tufted, and enjoys protected status, perhaps we should be pleased that there is so little habitat overlap.

The goldeneye

The final photograph shows the handsome goldeneye, a bird commonly found in estuary and firth. It flies very rapidly, low over the water, with a softly whistling wingbeat, and as it feeds heavily on such crustaceans as the shore crab it is rarely seen away from its open water habitat. The drake is very distinctive, with a great deal of white in the plumage, whilst the duck is duller with white wing bars. A very quiet species apart from the occasional gutteral growl. Other sea duck are to be found, all of which are now protected. Scoters, eiders and long-tailed are all fascinating species, but will be encountered but rarely except in more northerly waters.

Goldeneye (Bucephala clangula).

THE SAWBILLS

Red-breasted merganser (Mergus serrator). *Protected*

The sawbills (*Mergus*) are well distributed and common enough to warrant inclusion. Ostensibly duck-like, with both illustrated species being mallard size or larger, on closer examination there is in fact scant room for error. Both species fly low on softly sizzling wings in classic sawbill elongated shape – head, neck, body and tail all in line. They are seldom found away from open water, where they feed on small fishes and the like, and present few identification problems after an initial sighting.

Goosander (Mergus merganser). *Protected*

THE WADERS

Sadly for the wildfowler only one pure wading bird – the golden plover – remains as a legal quarry; even then this species can hardly be thought of as a shore wader, which at least makes identification relatively simple.

The golden plover

Habitat association is a valuable aid here, for the goldie will spend the greater part of its time on the marshland and upland fields feeding on invertebrates; some good flighting may be enjoyed as the birds leave the fields to head for some secondary roost on the open shore. Winter plumage lacks the black face and underparts of breeding birds, with the near white underside being a good first aid to identification, although black flecks may still remain. Sharply pointed wings, with pure white undersides are an easily noticeable feature, whilst the gold-spangled upper plumage loses much of its finery during the winter. Often seen in huge flocks, it flies swiftly and is thus highly rated as a sporting bird. The call is a delightful double fluted whistle.

*Golden plover (*Pluvalis apricaria).

The grey plover

Photographs of both golden and grey plover appear, with the grey mounted in the flying mode to clearly identify the black axillaries (armpits) which are most noticeable. Habitat association separates the species conclusively for the most part, with the grey only leaving the shore for the period of the high tide roost and even then it will seldom go farther than the nearest high salting or inland field. The voice of the grey plover is one of the most evocative sounds of the estuary – being a drawn out wailing plaintive whistle.

*Grey plover (*Pluvalis squatarola). *Protected*

The curlew

Two other waders are shown, as much for their common presence as anything else, although both species are the very personification of bird life on the shore. The curlew is quite unlike any other

Curlew (Numenius arquata). *Protected*

Oystercatcher (Haematopus ostralegus). *Protected*

species – save for the smaller summer migrant whimbrel (*N.phaeopus*). A huge brown, long-legged bird, armed with a great scythe of a downward curving bill, it gorges itself in the freshmarsh and on the open flats and will be seen flighting in vast, almost ducklike packs, to and from the shore. The melodic call from which its English name is derived is one of THE sounds of the shore.

The oystercatcher
The oystercatcher is a noisy and spectacular part of our winter scene, and can be seen flighting at the behest of the tide in great packs of loudly twittering birds. It is noted for the densely packed high tide roosts, and its disconcerting habit of looking like low-flying duck when approaching head on! The oystercatcher is another of those unique shore birds which soon become commonplace to every wildfowler.

SNIPE

Snipe (Gallinago gallinago).

The final pair of photographs depict the quarry common snipe, and the protected jack snipe. The snipe is classified as a game bird rather than a wader, and as such a Game Licence will be needed if one wishes to shoot this species. It is one of our most widely distributed and known birds, being found where ever there is a damp place which may harbour invertebrate prey. Its ruffous plumage and sharp 'shrap' call are easily identified by any shooting man. Invariably found in singles or odd wisps comprising a handful of birds, it can less commonly be found in larger concentrations – usually brought about by hard weather. Although an erratic flyer when first flushed, in level flight it is not especially swift, with its small size likely to cause range judging problems for the less experienced. It is easily distinguished from such similar size birds as dunlin (*Calidris alpina*) by the huge downward pointing bill, while it is very vocal when on the wing. The great snipe (*G.media*) occurs but rarely in the U.K. and need concern the wildfowler but little. The bill is shorter than the common snipe, while it is slightly larger in size – as the name suggests; it possesses conspicuous white markings on the tail, while is a fairly quiet bird.

Jack snipe (Lymnocryptes minima). *Protected*

In common with many shore waders, the jack snipe received protection in 1982. A tiny trusting bird it is smaller in stature and has a shorter bill than the common, and is far quieter; the suicidal habit of landing again close by after being flushed meant that it was easily bagged, and few sportsmen would argue about its protected status. Found less commonly in the saltmarsh it is a bird not easily confused with the common snipe despite the name.

The above gives an impression of life on the shore, but it is only a part of a complex and intricate story. The shore abounds with life and hopefully the above will serve as an appetiser for those with an initial interest; if so that which follows will represent a tale well worth the telling and illustrate how sport can be reconciled with a deep love of Nature's work on the coast.

—5—

Into October

FOR THE GREAT, black-looking, melanistic cock pheasant which flew from the saltings as the tide flooded strongly, this was to be the last day of carefree living for some four months. October First was but a few brief hours away, and thus the opening of yet another pheasant shooting season. The keeper would be busy about the marshes, feeding the birds and keeping the vermin in check. Soon the hopeful line of Guns would assemble and the drives would begin; drives aimed at putting birds such as this big melanistic into the bag, if he should be reckless enough to fly within range of the Guns. But he was a wily old cock; a bird of the saltmarsh, and therefore less likely to get caught up in one of the formal drives. He was far more likely to fall prey to some solitary gunner, with his keen-nosed dog questing the salting ahead.

As the day began to fade I watched the cock stand atop the seawall. He carried with him an air of regal grace: his head held high, his bulky form outlined against the western sky. Then he began to strut along the seawall, here and there pausing briefly to gulp down some titbit which he had found, eventually disappearing out of sight along the wall. He rather reminded me of one of those flashy bird-watchers.

October First shoot

October brought with it the first organised shoot on the great freshmarsh, and as I had a Gun in the syndicate of the day I deemed it proper to attend – even if I did so more out of courtesy than great enthusiasm. The term 'organised' is officially used by the shoot captain and his cohorts to describe such forays; I confess that I find the term 'disorganised' to be a far more accurate description. It never ceases to amaze me that no matter how meticulous the pre-shoot planning, the day invariably develops into something approaching chaos. However, I must quickly concede that I would not like to bear the responsibility for the day's proceedings; far better to say little, keep a low profile, and hope to keep one's end up with the gun.

One thing soon becomes apparent: some men are obviously born leaders; still others are born to be led, whilst some seem quite impossible to lead – seemingly destined to misunderstand the simplest of instructions. All good clean fun if you are not the unfortunate organiser. It is not always easy to keep a low profile. The performance with the gun will seldom go unnoticed: if one shoots too much there may be accusations of being greedy, whilst if one shoots too little it may be a case of letting the side down. It can be a problem. Such days are also noted for the fact that some unruly wildfowling dog is bound to break ranks and run amok, so the trick is to ensure that your dog is not the transgressor – even if this means keeping it on a lead. So keep a middle line by doing as asked both quickly and efficiently, and generally give the appearance of being a model Gun.

On this first day things did not go well right from the start. A late start, caused by the late arrival of several Guns – yours truly included – was bad enough, but the gaping holes in the line caused by the complete non-appearance of several regulars, plus guests, were big enough for whole coveys of partridges to slip through with ease. To anyone who knows anything of walking early season marshes with abundant tangled cover, the story will no doubt be a familiar one. Those carefully worked out plans had to be abandoned; this meant that there were no drives as such, and the day developed into one massive walk-up operation. Sport was thus much poorer than had been expected, and the organisers were very disappointed at the end of the day.

Alternative plans were laid at infrequent intervals, and as such plans seemed to alter with greater speed than the F.T. Index, we unfortunates on the far end of the line were entitled to feel a little peeved. The result was that we turned for the home lap, and a well earned lunch, with comparatively little in the bag. I had been foolish enough to shoot a large hare, whilst still some two hours from the lunch break, so that by the time we reached the cars I was pleased to have shot nothing else.

The afternoon was a little better, if only because we had less ground to cover, and I even managed to shoot a partridge myself. A very satisfying shot it was too, as the single bird rose in front of me with the wind in its tail, and it was over 40 yards out before I put the pattern into it. It was one of those awkward angled shots where one has to shoot under and to one side – my only bird of the day, but it could have scarcely been a better one. The ground game were very difficult to see in thick cover, so that it was a case of snap-shooting at close, fast targets. Those with dogs did best, for the animals would not bolt unless in danger of being trodden on, and we must have walked over a great many more than we actually flushed.

So the organised shoot ended, with the bag being divided. As always, some got more than they shot, some got less, but then such things generally even themselves out over the course of a season. The total bag to 14 Guns was: 40 rabbits, 12 partridges, five hares and two mallard. At last! The delights of being freed from the shackles of the shoot. Indeed, thoughts of the evening flight had been uppermost in my mind for much of the day as there was a raging gale blowing, and at one time I had seen a fair number of duck down by the seawall. If, as I suspected, they were roosting in the sheltered water I might be able to enjoy some good sport. As I made my way down through the marsh the sea was a raging maelstrom of white water, even though the tide was now on the ebb and this was likely to produce a calming effect as the tide ran with the wind instead of against it. This is one of those instances of secondary roosting which I mentioned earlier, and as such I have no qualms at shooting a few birds if the opportunity arises.

Evening flight
The wide fleet, which lay in the shelter of the low earthen seawall, was often a favourite with duck. The shallow margins were full of seed-bearing sea club rush, whilst much weed lurked below the waterline; as such several species of duck were apt to come to feed at various times, whilst the becalmed waters often provided a viable alternative to the storm-lashed waves. There was still a fair bit of weed and scum on the surface, a legacy of a dry long summer, but nevertheless there remained abundant open water, and from this half-a-dozen teal rose at my approach. With the water-level being fairly low it was an easy matter to use the cover of the tall sedges, backed by the long grass on the fleet edge, as a rudimentary hide, reasoning that so long as I kept my head down if any birds came near I would remain reasonably unobtrusive. Under such circumstances the use of a few decoys will prove immensely useful. In tidal conditions the larger the 'flock' the better; but in such an inland situation as this fleet, with the birds often heading for a

pre-determined destination, the token gesture of some half-a-dozen full-bodied decoys is usually sufficient.

If there had been a lot of birds on the fleet I might have expected plenty of action, but the six teal had proved something of a disappointment. At best I hoped for a few shots at flight-time, with perhaps two or three birds in the bag. Mediocre early season sport often induces a sort of pessimistic apathy in the wildfowler: because sport has been poor he tends to accept this as the norm, especially in the absence of any clear indication that the contrary might be the case. So it was this day, for I had only a few cartridges with me, and really saw no reason to worry on that score. How wrong can you be.

Even as the first pair of decoys splashed into the centre of the fleet I saw a pair of low-flying duck approaching from the sea; no time to add the rest of the flock; instead it was a case of ducking into cover and hoping for the best. They came straight on in with total confidence, so that when I showed myself they were very close and began to climb away right-handed with the wind making escape difficult for them. In truth, they were two fairly easy shots and I killed them both, one splashing into the water, with the second falling amongst the sedges on the nearside of the fleet. Thus two straight-forward retrieves for the dog who presented me with a pair of shoveler – my first shoveler of the season.

The launching of the second pair of decoys prompted the appearance of three wigeon, and these too came on purposefully beating in against the wind. I let them right in before killing a fine young cock as he turned across my front with broad white belly flashing in the clear sunlight; he too fell into the fleet, to float belly up before the dog swam out for him. A lone shoveler, intent on the

decoys but alarmed at the sight of the swimming dog, tried to use the wind to its advantage as it turned back. It was a testing shot, but I managed to clip it down with a broken wing; it fell into long grass, but was soon found and summarily despatched. What a beginning! At length I managed to get the third pair of decoys out, and sat back for a respite.

Four teal now approached, sweeping low over the marsh almost like fast-flying little fighter planes. A couple of encouraging nasal calls before they saw the decoys and came straight on in, so that they were almost on the water before they saw me. Of all our sporting birds the teal is arguably one of the best, with its speed of flight and amazing climbing ability when alarmed. But once the bird has lost that onrushing momentum it is reduced to more mortal proportions, and becomes no more difficult to kill than any other bird. This was now the case. I had them cold, with even the wind unable to help them as they climbed from zero feet, searching the teeth of that gale so that they could go racing away backed by its invisible force. I put the little automatic onto the first bird, and as it folded it was not difficult to keep the gun moving left-handed and upwards searching for the right and left. The second bird fell also, as did a third as I kept the gun moving sweetly; then the lone survivor had the gale in its wings, and flicked off downwind with incredible speed. I watched it go with some admiration – good luck little bird, I thought, I wish you well. The true worth of the moment hit me then as I saw the three dead teal floating in the fleet. It had been a useful piece of shooting, with scarcely 20 feet separating the three bodies. This was my first hat-trick at teal, and to be sure there can be few greater delights for the wildfowler. It was a slightly bemused dog that was obliged to make three successive trips into the water, whilst I stood idly by to applaud her work.

At last something of a respite, and time to consider what might have happened had I arrived a little earlier. A single wigeon then interrupted this idle musing; in fact I made the error of letting it in too close, so that it was an almost impossible shot at point-blank range as it turned across me. The second shot saved the day, sending it plummetting into the fleet some way off. Immediately three more wigeon, this time ignoring the decoys and my calling, crossed further down the fleet. When it was obvious that they could not be lured I fired a single shot at the rearmost, and saw it come spinning down like some giant sycamore twist, tumbling backwards in the gale before landing quite dead in the water. Two more easy retrieves for the dog.

Now something of a dilemma, for the cartridge situation was

becoming desperate, with the evening flight some way off. After a good deal of agonising I decided to take only the easiest shots, spurning such chances as the broken-winged shoveler and that last wigeon; in this way I hoped to make the most of the situation before I ran out completely. Inevitably the next three chances were all at extreme range, so I let them go – and after that the birds stopped coming. I sat about waiting for the light to fade, hoping that the evening flight would bring more birds to the fleet. Some brief speculation as to why the flight had ended as it had was probably answered in two ways: firstly the ebb tide had eventually uncovered the mud flats, thereby giving the duck an alternative safe roost; secondly, at such an early stage in the season there were comparatively few birds about anyway. Had this situation occurred a few weeks later the flight into the marsh may well have involved hundreds of birds. Still, I was not about to complain, even when the evening produced nothing save a couple of missing chances, for I had done exceptionally well. To come away with 10 duck under such circumstances was good going; nevertheless the perfectionist in me said that I should have had 15 or so, and perhaps I should. 10 is probably enough though.

Decoying duck in broad daylight in such easy surroundings as the fresh marsh is quite a treat for the foreshore wildfowler. One of the great advantages being the condition of the birds, for on the shore they invariably become splattered in mud which tends to mar their appearance somewhat. But on the marsh it is totally different, for they will mostly be brought to hand in pristine condition, unless some blood be present; thus it is possible to enjoy the slain in all their finery, and to feel an added reverence for these fine birds in the process.

Even with a slightly reduced wind there was plenty of reason for optimism on the morrow, and I hurried back to the fleet hoping, perhaps over-optimistically, for a repeat performance. This time I arrived very early, and well laden with cartridges, but predictably things were a lot quieter. Admittedly I did manage to get another six duck, five of which were wigeon, but I shot three of these on the evening flight – for now this tiny secondary roost was not needed.

Truly the freshmarsh is a glorious place, but soon pales into near-insignificance when compared to the foreshore. If the wigeon were already about in good numbers then it seemed logical to try a tideflight on the saltings at the earliest opportunity. The chosen place was a tiny spit of high ground which jutted out into a bay in the saltings; here I knew the tide would not reach, whilst there was a fair chance of getting a shot or two as the tide flooded. A pair of decoys set out from the spit might prove useful, and once the tide was up they looked realistic enough. Yet with little more than a gentle breeze blowing, the duck were content to loaf offshore in peaceful lines bobbing on the gentle swell. It was a glorious afternoon, if scarcely good wildfowling weather.

At length four mallard swung around the bay, prompted by my calling; one landed fairly close by, whilst the other three went off on another wide circuit out over the sea. I did not expect them back, so the chance at a wood pigeon was used in the hope that the shot might stir some of the loafing duck. I killed the pigeon easily enough, but the resultant confusion turned out better than I had expected. The mallard close by of course departed rapidly in the other direction, but the other three seemed disorientated by both the shot and my continued calling and duly headed straight for me. It was a long shot by any standards, but as I sat up to fire they swung slightly closer and I was able to bring down a handsome drake. He balled up in the manner of a dead bird, and hit the salting with a resounding thwack. A most satisfying shot. After that I lay back in the long grass largely disinterested in shooting any more duck. The drake lay nearby, an absolute riot of colour amongst the green of the salting grass, whilst the breeze whispered through the coarse stems ever so softly.

How, I wondered idly, could anyone dismiss the shore as being cold and unfriendly, and devoid of beauty. Obviously they do not really know the shore, nor are they able to appreciate it at such moments when the sun floods all beneath with its dazzling radiance. Indeed on this day I had seldom seen the salting look so beautiful, for it was ablaze with colour. At times the salting may seem a world of brown and green, but this day there was a wonderful fusion of so many different shades highlighted by the sun, so that even the straw shades of dead grasses took on a golden sheen. Further away lay a wide smudge of purple where the sea lavender grew, and this added an extra flavour to the scene.

Close by lay a tiny beach, no more than five or six paces wide. It had been created in a small break in the high clay banks of the salting, and was a wonderful mixture of shell where the waves had washed time without number. The sun burst down upon the beach, which sparkled back in a host of yellow and cream and white; the water itself was a deep blue, almost Mediterranean in its clarity, so that the whole place seemed as though it was from another world. I found an old broken-stemmed clay pipe cast over the ridge of the beach; it was white and insipid-looking, bleached by countless days lying there under the sun. I became almost transposed in time, with only the slowly grazing cattle on the seawall serving to remind me of the reality of the situation. It was a scene of rare beauty, and one which I felt privileged to have witnessed.

It was with a degree of sadness that I picked the decoys and made my way back to the seawall. I am basically an old-fashioned sort of chap, inclined to enjoy the simple things in life; a bright sun playing on a saltmarsh may be simplicity itself, but it can be incredibly beautiful – yes, I most certainly enjoyed this particular natural phenomenon. I waited by a fleet near the seawall for the duck which were not coming. At deep dusk I heard the nasal cronk of greylags; soon they were directly overhead, invisible against the void, and I listened to them as they pressed on to the east and some safe roost before the dawn once again brought the feeding urge to them. Soon small packs of wigeon began flighting in past my position, their gleeful whistling reminding me of so many winter nights on the shore. These were just the forerunners of the teeming thousands which were destined to follow, and as such I welcomed them – halcyon days lay ahead.

Somewhere close by the piercing whistle of a cock wigeon at rest, and after he had called a few times I knew where he must be. It was an easy enough stalk, even if it necessitated a long detour to avoid being silhouetted; every now and then I rested, until his whistle told me he was still there, then pressed eagerly on in my attempt to put him in the bag with the gaudy mallard. The stalk was all but over, for no further cover remained. I was in a dry ditch, not 20 yards from the main fleet from whence the cock was calling, and I slumped against the bank recovering my composure and listening to the periodic call. I was quite spellbound for I had never been this close to a calling cock wigeon before. The cock wigeon draws his whistle from deep inside, almost as if he were drawing on some hidden reserve of tundra air, then, preceded by a short rush of wind, the call is developed into the magnificent bursting whistle we all know so well. I lay there for long moments locked in an inner turmoil – should I complete the stalk, or let him be to live for another day. His whistle seemed to epitomise his mastery of the air and that unmistakable joy for life that was undoubtedly his. But the advantage was his, for it was pitch dark by now, and even if I put him up I should be lucky to get the chance of a worthwhile shot.

Then I was over the top of the ditch, rather like some desperate infantryman pushing off to meet the enemy wire, and hurrying, bent low down, for the fleet. A glimmer of clear water, and in that same instances came the splash of departing birds and the tell-tale flurry of wings: I stopped instantly, crouching with the stock of the gun tucked in tightly against my ribs, searching for a glimpse against the blackness of the seawall. Then there were surprisingly three of them, now above the seawall and racing for the security of the sea from whence they had come. The first shot missed, no doubt well behind, but I vaguely saw a bird fold at the second attempt and heard it hit the ground on the far side of the fleet with a satisfying thump.

After a good deal of shouting I managed to get the dog off a moorhen that had been skulking in the sedges close by, and set her to the wigeon. In a thrice she was swimming back, and soon presented me with a handsome adult cock, his plumage unruffled, with just a bright spot of blood at the bill. I felt a momentary pang, but he had been given every opportunity to escape – it was my good fortune and his bad luck that I had cat's eyes! I tucked him away with the mallard, and took him on his last journey as I headed for the car. He would call no more.

—6—

The Foreshore

I HAVE ALWAYS FIRMLY believed that the definition of the true wildfowler is the man who pursues his sport below the seawall, on the foreshore. He that hunts his fickle quarry over that wildest of lands, constantly exposed to the unremitting cruelty of the worst that nature can offer and the creeping danger of a flooding tide, can truly consider himself a wildfowler; he can walk with pride for in all honesty there are few sportsmen of his ilk. He is one of an elitist band of men. Yet the wildfowler should feel no shame if he chooses to sample the sort of inland sport which I have related, for it is a rather gentle way of enjoying a sport which has few shortcuts. Indeed, most wildfowlers possess many masochistic traits, and are often inclined to find the most difficult way of carrying out their sport. In this I am no exception, and tend to subscribe to the view that a little suffering aids the ultimate enjoyment of the sport.

In Chapter 4 I wrote something of the composition of the shore and the quarry. As most of what follows will occur on the shore this seems an opportune time to discuss some of the problems to be encountered there, although not so much in the sporting sense. In many ways sport must be considered less than the number one priority, in the first instance, even if this may seem a particularly curious statement to make, and consequently hard to accept for he who will in all probability be bursting with enthusiasm to get down to the shore and shoot some duck.

Much earlier I made the point about pre-season reconnaissance, and it is not really possible to overstate the importance of this. Even once the season has started it will be prudent for the budding wildfowler to spend any quiet duckless days learning all about the shore. Most experienced wildfowlers, perhaps visiting an area for

Typical saltmarsh creek.

the first time, should not need my bidding to make them aware of the reality of the situation: the foreshore can kill, and for the foolhardy or naïve the danger is a very real one, but for he who realises that a potential danger exists there should be less prospect of coming to grief – simply because he is more aware. This is not to say that every piece of foreshore is likely to prove lethal, whilst many exude an appearance of friendliness which may, in some cases, be real, but in others a dangerous illusion. My earlier example of flat, featureless *zostera* beds is meant to illustrate this last point, and I believe it does so quite adequately. Most certainly no sane person should disregard the advice relating to the use of a compass.

Many estuaries and coastal areas possess a complex system of mudflats, creeks and fragmented saltmarsh islands, and there are some particularly fine examples of this in Kent, where this book is based. A good deal of our wildfowling will, of necessity, take place in the depths of the saltmarsh, on the tide edge, or on some exposed salting island – quite simply because this is where the sport is to be had on the majority of occasions. Even the most complex of saltmarshes may seem innocuous enough at low tide, when the water may be way off into the distance and perhaps no more than a faintest of stirrings in the back of one's consciousness. But always remember that the tide will be back soon enough, and will have not a moment's hesitation in drowning whatever may lie in its path – whether this be man or mosquito.

Low tide

But firstly let us consider the foreshore at low tide. Although the absence of water may be a great help for someone wishing to get about on the shore, it would be rash to disregard any likelihood of danger. Quicksands and mud holes do exist, but even common or garden estuary mud can be quite a daunting prospect for many. There will be various techniques which the sportsman will need to use if he is to get about with the minimum of fuss and, where a great deal of mud-walking is involved, unless he quickly learns how to deport himself he will find wildfowling a sweaty nightmare. To the experienced man the sight of an eager novice floundering hopelessly in some muddy quagmire may be an amusing one, especially if the end result be the loss of one, or even both, waders. But there will be nothing funny about this experience for the unfortunate person on the receiving end, so that a few words of advice would be a good substitute for ridicule.

The loss of a wading boot can be largely avoided by ensuring that they are securely tied in place, and most makes have straps to tie around the waist. Waist fixings are all well and good unless one is likely to encounter some really deep and glutinous mud – the sort of stuff often to be found in creeks and gutters – in which case it will be necessary to tie cord or wire around the ankles. This will have the effect of preventing too much give as the boot is withdrawn, and in this way better progress should be possible. Of course, the main substantial drawback with ankle straps is that on those exceedingly rare occasions when shedding a boot is the only way of escaping from a really sticky patch it will probably be quite impossible to do so. So it will be necessary to balance one likely problem against another; personally, having developed a fair degree of proficiency in mud, I prefer to opt for ankle straps every time.

Mud walking on surfaces of a fairly even consistency – say mud no more than ankle deep – can be very energy sapping, and it is often a question of determination to overcome this problem as much as it is one of stamina. The secret of this type of walking is to keep moving, if at all possible, at a steady pace; better this than to dash off like an Olympic sprinter, only to finish a shattered wreck after the first 100 yards! Walk with the weight on the ball of the foot, rather than flat-footed, as this will reduce suction as the foot is drawn up for the next step. If it becomes necessary to stop for more than a few seconds, whether for a rest or some other reason, never make the elementary mistake of striding off again in impetuous fashion. The near-certain result of this will be that the feet have become firmly stuck and you will end up full length in Nature's stickiest! Always loosen each foot before restarting the journey. Even really stodgy mud, such as the exit from deep creeks, must be tackled aggressively and with optimum speed, for in this way the likelihood of becoming bogged down will be much reduced. If the worst happens and you do become stuck in deep mud, it may be necessary to lie over backwards to pull free; this is inevitably a very messy business, but infinitely preferable to waiting for the next tide.

Anyone who does any amount of mud and salting work will consider a stout wading pole as a fundamental piece of their equipment. Such an aid will not only find a use for plumbing water depth, but will be useful to aid the crossing of dried-out creeks, and will generally make mud-walking that much easier. Such a pole can be a great comfort and help when stodgy patches are chanced across; the dog too may well prove a lifesaver one day, for a hand upon a strong neck may be all that is needed to pull oneself free.

If I have painted an austere picture of the dangers of mud I have not done so unnecessarily, rather out of a keenness to see others become aware of the problems involved. Also when I write of keeping up a good steady pace on mud I do so in the realisation that not all are of my build, so that what may be relatively easy for my 10½ stone may be an entirely different matter for someone who may be four or five stones heavier.

Of course not all mud will be of the same depth, with substantial variations often occurring within a matter of a few yards. Often there will be no clearly discernable difference to the eye, but on many occasions vital clues will be available to guide the experienced man away from the worst areas. Invariably the creek rims will consist of hard compacted mud, whilst even a stride to one side will prove a totally different proposition; similarly, heavily rippled mud will often be reasonably firm to walk over, even if it may prove something of a horror after dark. Frequently where vegetation such as *zostera* grows, the mud will be more likely to be reasonably stable and safe to walk on; however, it pays to quickly learn the difference between vegetation and algae, as algae-covered mud is often very soft indeed. Other soft spots are likely to occur at any place where some sort of barrier exists, such as a jetty or seawall,

Using a wading pole for crossing a deep creek.

because here the tidal flow will have been impaired and invariably dangerous silts will have accumulated; a strong tidal flow will seldom allow the build-up of silts and sediments, and therefore the mud is likely to be a great deal firmer. The above goes some way towards indicating the many variations likely to be found on the mud of the foreshore, and serves to re-emphasise the need for a thorough understanding of your chosen shore. But it will also pay to bear in mind that muds can change from season to season – indeed such changes do even occur within a single winter – so be prepared for this eventuality.

High tide
The saltmarsh itself will probably be relatively harmless at low tide, with only the creeks and gutters liable to cause any problems, it is once the tide has turned that the wildfowler must look to his laurels if he wishes to avoid coming to grief. All saltmarsh islands and many main saltmarshes will become cut off from the seawall during the high tide period, and the wildfowler must familiarise himself with a number of points before he ventures out. If he wants to shoot over the saltings around the high tide period, and this can sometimes be the most productive of times, he must establish: (a) the height of the tide, (b) any high points on the marsh which may enable him to sit out that height of tide, and (c) what, if any, effect will the prevailing weather conditions have on this particular tide. Now there is an interesting little parcel to consider, but this must be done accurately for it really may prove to be a case of life and death.

This making tide will soon cut you off.

Local knowledge is once again the key. For example in the Medway Estuary most saltmarshes will be safe on the neap (smallest) tides, with little, if any, of the established marsh going under at high tide. A great number of the saltings will be fairly secure even on the medium height tides, so that only when you reach the springs (the largest tides) will the majority go under; it therefore follows that the Kentish wildfowler must know which islands will remain dry once we are up to some 6.2+ metres of tide, and there will be precious few of these. Many of these islands and saltmarshes seem substantial areas with towering clay embankments at low water, but come high water there will be surprisingly little greenery left. To the uninitiated this may come as something of a shock, and should certainly serve to temper any runaway enthusiasm with a hint of realism. So the height of the tide will dictate which if any, marshes are tenable at high water.

If the sportsman wishes to avoid a lengthy spell isolated from the mainland, whether through choice or for safety reasons, he must be sure to leave himself plenty of time to cross any creeks which might bar his way once the tide is in full flood. Therefore he must learn how long after low water he can afford to stay on the marsh before being obliged to beat a safe retreat; this may vary considerably and by anything from one to three hours after low water, although the common factor will normally prove to be the speed with which such creeks will fill once the flood has begun. Such a creek may seem a pitiful affair when empty, but once filling with grubby brown water sweeping in from the estuary, it will seem a different matter entirely. Saltmarsh creeks, even the relatively

94

small ones, have a great penchant for being both too wide to leap and too deep to wade, and more than one wildfowler in the past has felt the sudden stab of fear as he finds his escape route cut off.

A local tide table is an absolutely essential part of any wildfowler's equipment, but he will be well advised to treat the predictions contained therein as nothing more than that – predictions, albeit of a very well-informed nature. Any wildfowler who treats the contents of the tide table as sacrosanct is heading for a nasty surprise before his days are over! Barometric pressure, if there is a marked variation between low and high pressure, can affect the actual height of the tide. Yet it is the wind which will have the most notable effect, and it is well known that a big spring tide together with an onshore gale can spell serious trouble for anyone out on the saltings. So, as I said earlier, the height of tide should not be considered in isolation.

A strong offshore wind can have the effect of either depressing the tide height or delaying the flood tide. Of course neither can be absolutely relied on, and neither will have the same killing potential as the onshore blow. The big onshore blow, and for east coast wildfowlers this basically means any north or easterly wind, can have a devastating effect. The tide can surge in much earlier than normal, whilst water piling in from the North Sea can put several feet on the height of the tide; in real terms this will almost certainly mean the complete inundation of everything below the seawall. In extreme cases, with the east coast floods of 1953 as the classic example, sea defences will be breached, many thousands of acres flooded, property destroyed and lives lost.

On a sleepy peaceful day the sea may seem a gentle and often beautiful part of Nature's creation. But on another day it can become a white-capped fury of unimaginable force the like of which must be seen to be believed. Beside the might of the sea most of Man's achievements will seem puny indeed – whilst the spectre of a lone wildfowler crouched on some rapidly shrinking island is a frightening one to say the least. Meteorological reports are readily available on a local basis at the turn of a telephone dial, and for a few pence we can obtain some sort of warning of impending bad weather. It is just one further simple pre-flight precaution which I heartily recommend, especially if a tide flight is planned on some exposed saltmarsh. But even though we sound dire warnings to others this does not necessarily mean that our words will be heeded. I even confess to thoroughly foolish and irresponsible behaviour myself, albeit many years ago when the flush of youth tended to make one a little blasé about the real value of life. Now I think back and cringe, and can think of an anecdote worth relating for it illustrates in a most graphic fashion what I have just been saying.

A friend and I determined to visit a local offshore island for the evening flight, and, although it was traditionally a place which produced the best results over high water, we knew that a brief hour or so when low water coincided with evening flight would be likely to produce a few shots. The place was beloved by teal, for it contained a good selection of those classic food plants outlined earlier, and in the right conditions could provide some superb sport. We knew that there would be little time to spare for the return journey, but if we were away quickly and did not hang about there would be sufficient time, even though access was via a long stony causeway which snaked out from the mainland. A fierce north-easterly raged in from the outer estuary so that it cut into any exposed flesh with the precision of a surgeon's scalpel, and the walk out into the teeth of that cruel gale was a torture for us both. We crossed the last drained-out creek and reached the foot of the island's crumbling seawall. This was a glorious experience, for the wind was completely blotted out and it allowed us the much appreciated opportunity of getting our breath back after the severe buffeting which we had been obliged to suffer. But we knew what to expect once this temporary windbreak was left behind. The wind seemed to shriek right down from the ice-laden Baltic, to tear at rasping lungs and pull and tug at any item of clothing which was in anyway insecure.

A few teal rose reluctantly from the interior of the island to batter their way seaward in a drunken tottering flight, and at an altitude to make any wildfowler's heart sing. The marsh lay before us like the bowl of some ancient crumbling coliseum, and we were eager to reach some sort of cover both as protection against the wind, and in order to get out of sight in anticipation of the evening flight. Hopefully those teal would return, and bring a few more with them. I found a deep, sheer sided creek, with an almost solid floor; this was an absolute luxury, for I was out of the wind and able to stand quite comfortably without sinking into the creek bottom. One of the great problems associated with this sort of shooting is that of becoming totally bogged down so that it is almost impossible to turn if a bird comes on the wrong side of you. Here this situation did not apply, for it was almost like standing at the covertside.

The sky was as clear and as cloudless as could be, and the prospect of sharply diving temperatures after dark, undoubtedly accelerated by a considerable wind-chill factor, would be an additional incentive to get off the marsh without excessive delay. It later transpired that the night was one of the coldest of that particular winter, and most certainly not suitable for sitting out on some windswept island. It was very dark, and the sun had long since vanished below the western horizon on its endless journey to bring light and life to other lands, before the first teal came back. When they did arrive it was as tiny swarming black bees from out of the gloom and wind of the east at quite frightening speeds; once into the marsh they went off on high speed circuits, in search of a suitable feeding area, before eventually fluttering down out of sight.

Eventually I got one as it quartered across the wind, for it to fall way behind me. Predictably the shot put up some of those that had landed back in the marsh and, as the usual escape route was past my position, I soon found a nice little pack bearing down on me. This time the advantage was all mine, for they were hugging the ground in an attempt to escape the worst effects of the wind, so that one was falling before they were even aware of my presence; there was just time to kill a second as they climbed before the wind scattered them upwards and backwards, and in a moment they were gone. Even as the dog was doing her bit, more teal came like bullets out of the gloom and I tried several ineffective shots. They were just too quick for me with the wind behind them, and it was quite impossible to estimate their speed. They could easily have been travelling at twice their normal speed or even more, which would have meant they were doing something in the region of 70–80 m.p.h.

I called one bird back and killed it as it flashed by with what was a very passable shot. How curious to see that tiny streamlined shape turn into a compact tumbling ball of feathers and shattered flesh, before flopping to the ground for the last time – there is great satisfaction in killing the target bird stone dead. My friend was shooting sparodically from his position off to the west, and on occasion this sent birds back past me although with the light all but gone it was difficult to see them approaching. At length I flicked one down with a broken wing, which gave the dog a fair old chase in the blacked-out saltings; at length she had the little hen bird, and brought it for me to despatch instantly with a snap of the neck. A curious unease had begun to grip me as the flight had been overtaken by the onset of night, and although there was nothing that I could put my finger on, I was glad to join my friend and hurry back across the marsh. This time the wind was at our backs, so that it was easier to hurry; a glance at the watch told us that we had plenty of time, but the strength of the wind and that nagging doubt in the back of the mind was enough to cause a quickening of the stride.

The golden rule for that marsh, with the two main creeks breaking the causeway at either end, is if there is flood water in either creek then there will not be time to cross the second before the tide is too deep. At least that was the theory, although I had never been entirely convinced that this was in fact the case. We reached the seawall and instantly the apprehension was explained, for there below us in the creek was the first shiny finger of the incoming tide. Damn the wind! The tide was almost an hour early, and an instant dilemma faced us: did we ignore that rule of thumb and attempt to get back; or did we stay on the island until the next safe period, some 10 hours hence.

The prospect of 10 hours on that freezing marsh, with no food or drink and only equipped for a one-hour evening flight, was far from pleasant; neither was the prospect of being trapped between the flooding creeks, or of a ducking at the inland end of the causeway. One thing was certain: there was no time for debate, for if we were to go we would need every second and also hope that the wind would push us on to an effective escape. At length we went down into the creek and noted that the tide was not yet over our ankles – and went. The half-walk, half-stumbling run through mud and over stones still made slippery by the bulbous bladderwracks, was like some endless, unremitting nightmare from which it is quite impossible to awaken. The stick alternately found soft mud, or flew wildly from some stone or rock, whilst the whole time the wind raged like some devilish fiend as though urging on man and tide in some macabre race. At last! The shore came in sight, looming blackly before us, yet a more welcoming sight it would be difficult to imagine: an instant later the delight was turned to horror as the creek appeared before us as a wide river rippling menacingly where the wind played across its surface. How deep was the barrier? How fast was the current?

Such questions were academic because we had to go across – there was no alternative. To someone like I who cannot swim, the thought of wading out into a wide, maybe bottomless, stretch of water in the dead of a winter's night is likely to be at best a deeply sobering experience! Perhaps the first few steps are not so bad, but as the ground falls away and the first of the ice-cold water pours into the thigh boots, any notion that this may be some romantic adventure straight out of the pages of wildfowling legend will be very swiftly dispelled. In those moments when the water reaches waist level, and still continues to rise, the notion that perhaps 10 hours back on that lonely island would not have been too bad after all passes endlessly through a frightened mind. The water came on, filling the pockets of my shooting coat, whilst the sideways pressure from the tide was now difficult to resist. Each step was fraught with danger, for even as the ground below levelled out, the tide tugged greedily at the feet in its attempt to knock me over. Had this happened I would most certainly have drowned, I have no doubt on that score, and this knowledge terrified me at the time and has caused my blood to run cold whenever I have considered the matter afresh. A moment of great danger was there and gone as one of the dogs swam into me, and for a moment I thought that I was about to go over. Then the water was receding, the tidal pressure reduced, and we were through. We were soaked to the skin and frozen, but alive and well and able to reflect on the error of our ways.

Ah! you may well say. But he lectures us on the correct mode of behaviour on the shore, only to do what is fundamentally wrong himself! I advise now not out of hypocrisy, but from the standpoint of once bitten twice shy. I was foolhardy in the extreme, but lived to tell the tale and to thus warn others. You may not be so fortunate, so heed this warning well!

—7—

Before the Frosts

ONCE OCTOBER IS well advanced and the first substantial numbers of migrant ducks are 'in', the wildfowler can begin to shrug off some of his early season slothfulness. Now there will be a new spring in his step and a renewed sense of enthusiasm for the sport; the shore will once again throw up new sights and sounds, whilst a sense of excitement will be regenerated. The nights have turned noticeably colder, even if more than the occasional frost is a rarity, whilst the daylight hours grow shorter and cooler. In many ways the end of British Summer Time represents an important turning point in the season, for thereafter it will be possible to go out for the evening flight yet still get home by a reasonable hour. Although the keeping of social hours has never bothered a wildfowler overmuch there can be no denying that early season evening flights, which often entail arriving home at almost midnight, can get a little wearing when an early start for work next day is necessary.

So as October draws on, the shore is a good place to be, for even in the absence of a sporting quarry there will be much to see as a whole host of migrants arrive. Wildfowl, waders, raptors and passerines all pile in to their over-wintering quarters in and around our estuaries, and given reasonable weather conditions this is where they will remain until it is time for the homeward migration in the spring. All in all a stimulating and interesting time. Even if regular habits have yet to establish themselves in newly arrived birds it is still worth getting down to the shore as often as possible in the hope of a shot or two. At this time anything can happen, and invariably does! Just now and then some excellent sport can be had, whilst there is always the likelihood of a bird – which is more than can be said for that earlier limbo time.

October evening flight

If during the early pages of this book I have given the impression of enjoying a high proportion of successful days, I should like to put the record straight and say that this is most certainly not the case. Rather the good days are both more interesting to write about and, I hope, better reading; yet for all that it is not crucial to put something in the bag in order to enjoy the day out, and if the reader thinks this another of the perversities of this sport he may well be right. Whether we be outdoor fanatics or not I can think of no obvious merits attached to being out in the rain. I have tried really hard in this connection, but to no avail; I do not cringe from the rain, but nevertheless do not like sitting out in it one bit. To demonstrate this point I describe one October evening flight.

The drive to the shore was conducted under dark, greying skies. No rain as yet, but obviously plenty not too far off, so I knew there would be scant opportunity for any worthwhile ornithology; this realisation found little favour with me, as I love such an opportunity, often arriving early just to watch the waders working the mudflats. As I was changing it came on to rain, so I left the binoculars in the car and stomped off along the seawall in rather grumpy fashion. Once actually on the saltings I found a wet hiding place on the edge of a wet creek, and settled my wet person in ambush for whatever wet and bedraggled birds might chance my way. The rain came sweeping in from the west and I sat and indulged in a good deal of self-pity and discontent.

While in the midst of this black depression a pair of teal sneaked up on me, almost catching me out. The hasty first shot was well behind, but as they went into that steep climb I knew the second shot was on target and even though the bird did not fold up it was obviously badly hit. The value of using an automatic was really hammered home as the stricken bird turned back towards me, so that I could kill it easily with the third shot. After that I took less notice of the rain and stopped feeling sorry for myself. Yet the feeling of alarm rose up again as the light began to fade and I realised with horror that I had forgotten my insect repellent; the avenging hosts, denied a decent meal for the last few weeks, attacked my upturned face with great ferocity, as if eager to make the most of my temporary aberration. One would expect heavy rain to discourage such anti-social behaviour, but the reverse seems to occur, certainly on this occasion there seemed to be no loss of appetite.

Blast those mosquitos. They hurt. Despite my experience I am ashamed to report that I allowed anti-mosquito tactics (i.e. swatting) to take precedence so that I was scarcely concentrating on the job in hand. This is usually a fatal thing to do, with any error likely to be compounded when facing the darkest part of the sky, as I was on this occasion. When the birds appeared from behind it was without any warning at all. All of a sudden they were there – 11 pintail – and of course I missed them; indeed such was my state of unreadiness I only managed to fire a single shot, despite the fact that they were barely 30 yards up and directly overhead. Thus the chance at pintail – for me the most coveted of all duck – was squandered. Having done the damage, the mosquitos retired, leaving me to curse my bad luck. But mostly you make your own luck; this blunder was definitely my own fault, for if I had not forgotten the repellent the insects would have been kept at bay, and perhaps I might have hit one of those pintail. On the other hand I might have missed anyway and been left with no excuse at all. I saw nothing else at all and when the night had closed right in, only a short while later, I trudged back with the rain still pounding down. Damn the rain. Damn the mosquitos. Roll on the harshness of the winter frosts which would make life too difficult for the voracious little brutes.

Learn and enjoy
The before evening flight study of birds has many benefits, most of which are admittedly aesthetic. But, of course, being the inquisitive creatures that we are there will always be that quest for knowledge,

be it ever so slight. Observation is a means of learning and it therefore follows that the more we watch the more we will learn. If we can learn and enjoy all in one then we are fortunate indeed.

One bright mild afternoon I skulked in the sedge-filled margins of a fleet close to the seawall. There were no duck and I did not really expect any, but there were plenty of snipe; in fact there were snipe everywhere – in the ditches, flying low overhead, or darting off over the seawall to the saltings. I had no intention of spoiling the moment by firing a shot, preferring to watch and savour an experience which might not be repeated again for many a long day. The sun highlighted the plumage of these ostensibly brown and uninteresting birds every time one flew near, turning the white belly and striped browns into a fascinating blend of pattern. Sometimes one would rise from nearby, where some trick of light may have caused it alarm, and go dashing away to the accompaniment of its harsh rasping call, indeed this distinctive sound formed the backdrop for most of the afternoon and served to highlight the extent of snipe movement.

Most exciting of all is to be able to view at really close quarters the onrushing dive of birds coming to the muddy margins of the fleet to feed: a rasping cry, a rush of tiny wings, and then the small bird is flashing low above the sedges before setting those slender matchstick legs into the shallows. A bird some 20 feet away is captured and magnified in the all-seeing lens of the binoculars, so that it is possible to see its every move in the minutest detail. Now that massive bill no longer seems out of place. Watch as the bird thrusts that bill deep into the gluey mud, seeking out some tasty invertebrate; then, with quick eager movements, the bill is worked backwards and forwards – typically from four to six times – in an effort to locate the food and extract it from its hiding place. Then the thrusting shaft will be withdrawn, the tip festooned in thick black mud, and with a quick jerk the morsel is swallowed. The procedure will be repeated immediately, sometimes from the same position, but equally often it will move on to a likelier looking spot. It is a fascinating study, but always it is a seemingly endless search for food.

One morning towards the end of the month I spotted a massive flight of mallard involving several hundred birds. They crossed the seawall well out of bounds, and thereafter flew right off past my position in a stream of flighting packs which lasted for over an hour. What was needed was a big westerly blow to keep them down, and the good fortune to have the flightline change a little to bring some of the birds within range of the salting edge. By chance within two days a raging westerly gale had built up, so that it was highly likely the mallard would be flying much lower, that was always assuming the flight had not already dispersed. Accordingly I set off before dawn filled with high hopes, and well laden with cartridges just in case.

Dawn flight
As dawn broke the first packs appeared, and even though many were flying very low indeed they had scarcely altered their line so that very few came anywhere near; instead they kept well out over the mud, which in turn was quite featureless and devoid of cover. It meant staying put and hoping to pick off any wayward birds. Soon a very big pack of wigeon came right through the salting and I cut one out, whilst the rest scattered like leaves before an autumn gale and were gone before I could fire again. Eventually I moved to a tiny exposed outcrop of salting in an effort to get another shot and this ruse worked instantly as a low pair came right to me, although it took me two shots to kill the drake. The flight over the mud had now developed into one of massive proportions, far more birds than I had seen on the previous occasion. They were mainly mallard, but included a few wigeon and teal, with the vast majority flying at little more than 20 feet from the ground – a heart-rending sight.

With no cover, not even the tiniest of gutters, and no spade with which to create my own, the prospect of lying out on the mud without being seen was negligible to say the least. The duck might be struggling against the wind and exceedingly low flying, but they were most definitely not stupid. Finally the frustration got the better of me – I just had to try something. At length I gathered a few lengths of driftwood and plowtered out across the mud almost to the tide edge, which was where I estimated the bulk of the flight to be crossing, and using the wood as a makeshift groundsheet lay down more in hope than anticipation.

If there had been poor light I may have stood a chance, but now in the full early morning light I stood out like the proverbial sore thumb. It was a real heartbreaker, for the birds would approach at little more than head height, then just when it seemed as though they had not seen me they would veer to one side or the other and pass on the limit of range. At length a pair pushed their luck and, although it was a long shot, I gave the front bird a huge lead and fired. The rearmost fell with a broken wing so after the retrieve I gave up in disgust. The flight continued even as I walked back, long smudging streaks in the now crisply clear sky of a new morning.

Under the circumstances I had done well to get three, and was able to muse ruefully on what might have been; still the wildfowler's store of knowledge had been added to, and just maybe if conditions ever repeated themselves I should be able to do much better. That was many years ago and with the area now an RSPB reserve this is one piece of information that is quite useless to me.

Practical considerations
In actual physical terms shooting on the foreshore can be as arduous and demanding a pastime as one is likely to find. Actual access can be a long-winded and energy-sapping business, as anyone familiar with negotiating estuarine mud will verify; even though we all eagerly look forward to each trip to the shore, there can be no denying that the completion of the return walk is also awaited with a fair amount of relish. I have already highlighted some of the problems associated with finding cover on the open shore, and mostly this will have to be contrived as there is little in the way of readily available natural cover. In the saltmarsh it is a different story; most certainly there will be abundant cover in the pre-Christmas part of the season, when the saltmarsh plants will be at their most luxuriant, although once the heavy frosts, snow and gales of January and February have done their work, the scene frequently reminds the onlooker of a sort of battlefield-type devastation.

Making use of natural cover

For flighting during the low tide period there will seldom by any need to take additional hide-building material. As most such areas will be a maze of wandering creeks of varying sizes it is an easy matter to sit on the edge of one of the shallow creeks, with the tall sea aster and *spartina* providing ample protection from sharp-eyed duck: as I highlighted previously, the feet will need to be on a lower level than the backside, both for comfort and ease of movement when taking a shot. Most experienced wildfowlers have learnt to shoot well from this sitting position, and this is something which any tyro will do well to emulate without delay. The ability to take any chance as it comes, frequently from a very awkward position, is fundamental to good effective wildfowling, and although some of the torturous gun positions adopted by wildfowlers would make any shooting school tutor cringe, good results are all that count at the end of the day. On the majority of occasions the saltings will provide sufficient cover to conceal the dog as well, but it may be prudent to take some small piece of netting to aid with this; personally I use my small sidebag to cover the dog where necessary, and even if she may groan a little at times I think she likes it really.

A brief description of one such trip to a distant flighting place may be beneficial as it will serve to highlight some of the points I have been making. For anyone that doubts any of my assertions about access problems on the shore may I suggest that they come with me now on a little 45 minute hike, but first be sure to tie your waders at the ankles and have a stout wading pole to hand.

The walk will consist of an initial 15-minute plowter through calf-deep mud until the first of the saltings are reached. Hope that the sun is not out to begin with, as the sweat will rise quickly enough as it is, and hope that the mud is not in one of its ultra-tacky phases, for it can vary enormously. Blessed relief is the salting, but it is at once cruel and kind for it can in places be a tantalising mixture of firm reassuring ground and cunningly soft patches of black stinking mud. Then the first big creek – a looming cavernous wound which runs out of the high saltmarsh and thereafter wanders in nonchalant fashion down to the low water mark. If the mud around the creek edges be firm then the sides are anything but, rather a slippery glutinous suction which tries to hold you fast at every step. The creek bottom may vary from rock hard to deep and treacherous, whilst the trickle of water serves as a reminder of the raging brown torrent which had gone this way only a short time before. Once into the creek bed there comes the problem of clambering out the other side, and if you have used any

The scramble for firmer ground.

commonsense at all you will have chosen a crossing point where the sides are less sheer.

Nevertheless it will be a breath-rasping, gut-wrenching experience, whilst the value of the wading pole will become amply demonstrated. Attack the exit with aggression and as much speed as you can muster, and even though the momentum will be quickly lost, it is imperative to keep moving if the wish is to avoid becoming bogged in. Once stuck halfway up a creek side it can be the very devil of a job to get going again.

At last the creek is behind, so that it is possible to lean for a moment with heaving sides on the much-abused wading pole. But look, already the sun is low in the western sky – come on, soon it will be time for flight. Only five more creeks to cross. The saltings which lie between the creeks are, in places, a maze of tiny gutters, whilst the soft patches are frequently too wide to jump, necessitating a slow zigzag route or else the direct commando-style attack – ploughing through everything as it comes. This latter method is, I suspect, not to be advised – even for commandoes. Even the level saltings, devoid of any such obstacles, will have other surprises in store, such as the tangle of bent and broken aster and *spartina* stems which will be guaranteed to sap the strength of the leg-weary traveller. The walk is akin to one giant obstacle course.

At last the relief of reaching the destination, so that the hot and near-exhausted visitor can sit in the grubby isolation of the saltmarsh and contemplate his surroundings for a while before the onrush of night. Yet no matter what the result of the flight, whether this be good, bad or indifferent, there is always the certain knowledge that the return trip must be made in pitch darkness. Now the wading pole really earns its keep, for without one there would be many spills, either on the slippery-sided mud lumps or in the gloom of the saltmarsh where the tiny gutters are almost invisible in the tangle of plants. Often any darker patch on the ground may be a gutter, and a swift poke with the pole will settle the issue, so that at length a rhythm can be established of probing the ground in front for obstacles – thereafter moving confidently forward.

On most nights true darkness does not come to the shore. For the experienced wildfowler this simply means that even if it is pitch dark to mere mortals it is still light enough for him to get about with relative ease; seldom is it really pitch black at night, and mostly this occurs on stormy rainy nights when even the experienced man will have problems. But for the non-believer that return trip in the dark, so casually dealt with by his wildfowling guide, will prove to be a seemingly interminable drag. The firmness of the road at journey's end is a delight, whilst such solid ground has a strange feel underfoot after spending so long locked in splay-footed combat with the shore.

During the period of the full moon, when the shore may be lit up like day, it will be a totally different matter. This is a time when it is possible to traverse formerly daunting obstacles with a gay abandon. Any detailed discussion of shooting in the moonlight can wait until later on, so here I shall content myself by saying that the moonlit shore is something entirely unique in sporting terms; there is a kind of magical aura attached to this aspect of the sport, and I know of none who can fail to be captivated by its splendour.

—8—

Inside the Saltmarsh

ONCE OCTOBER IS LEFT behind the enthusiasm, of which I wrote at the opening of the last Chapter, becomes redoubled, for November and December in the South-East will be the time for the best of our sport. Obviously there will be plenty of exceptions to this rule, but for good consistent sport this period will normally come up trumps.

The period of the November moon – I believe it is known in some parts as the Hunter's moon, and quite rightly so – is when many migrants reach these shores, seemingly using the extra light to show them the way across the seas. Invariably it is also the time of the first real frosts, so that at last we are able to accept something of the flavour of the real winter without its taste being tainted by some bitter pill. This will also be the time, unless one is very unfortunate indeed, when some of the most evocative aspects of foreshore sport can be experienced. There are several natural phenomena which I believe epitomise the very essence of wildfowling, and of these I shall write a little before these pages are completed; whether I can succeed in sharing the wonder of these experiences with the reader, via the written word, only he can judge, but it will be well worth the attempt even if I only partially succeed.

Of these natural spectacles two are so bold and brash as to be impossible to ignore: the first is the massed flight of the wigeon flocks as they head inland to feed upon the rich pickings of the inland floods, whilst the second is the wild, noisy flight of the grey geese as they come down from the fields to roost either on the flats or out on the edge of the sea. These flights are an incredible experience, and will leave an indelible mark on any that chance to be a witness. Two further examples possess a measure of subtlety to such an extent that perhaps only the wildfowler, ensconsed in watchful solitude on the saltmarsh, may be aware that they exist at all. I write of the madcap onslaught of the teal when they come to the saltmarsh to feed at deepest dusk; also I write of the time when the tiny snipe decide that the salting is to their liking, and in consequence they rush there in untold numbers at the very death of the day. In many ways the time of the teal and that of the snipe have similarities, yet they are at once totally different.

November snipe

One afternoon I sat alone, save for the faithful dog, on the very edge of the saltmarsh in that area where the sea aster breaks down and the salting becomes diffused and more complex; where solid higher parts alternate with stodgy lower levels; where the mud is black and festooned with algae, and where the samphire grows to be littered all about with millions of the tiny *hydrobia*. This is the place where the teal often come, but is also a haven for the snipe that so adore this sticky, smelly stratum and the abundance of invertebrate life to be found there. Thus November is a good time to be in this place, for many birds may be attracted by the food on offer. Mallard too may come to sample the riches of the salting edge, so that even on a modest day there may be an interesting variety of birds about. It is a useful time to get down to some serious sport at last.

It was a typical November afternoon, cloudless and with scarcely a breath of wind so that the sky took on a blue of amazing and almost breathless clarity. It was the sort of sky against which birds would be very difficult to see once the light began to fade, with only the western horizon presenting a reasonable opportunity for picking out any incoming birds. As ever, I sat facing the west as the sun vanished to leave its dying embers burning low down in the sky; for a while the saltings seemed almost alight, whilst a short distance away a small mud pan shone briefly until the glow began to fade and dark shadows began to enfold the shore. It was good to see one or two teal about, though none came near enough for a shot, and for a while I held out hopes that perhaps this would be the night when the teal would come at last – but it was not to be, and I was scarcely surprised for the 'feel' was not in the air. This 'feel' is a curious thing, almost like a sixth sense possessed by so many hunting men. It really does exist, of that I am quite sure, and no doubt there are many fellow sportsmen who could confirm what I say; it is not some fanciful notion dreamt up by such as I, and although it is at best unreliable, there will be times when much use can be made of it.

A single low-flying bird was almost on me before I saw it, and was point-blank when I fired so that it fell like a broken rag doll behind me. It turned out to be a fine drake shoveler, not a terribly common bird on the saltmarsh, and as such I was doubly pleased. Now with the light fading fast the salting was mostly quiet, save for the occasional tearing of wings where the odd lone teal tore past to some secret table further along the shore. Somewhere far up in the blacked out sky came the stuttering chatter of a mallard pack, whilst the barely audible sighing of their pinions floated down to me.

High up came the sharp rasp of a snipe, then again much closer. A moment later the tiny bird hurtled past, far too quickly for a shot, before landing a few yards away in some slushy patch. Now was the time to become ever more alert, for the chance of a snap-shot was always there, though by now the light was very bad for attempting to get onto such a small quarry. Soon another came with the same rasping call; a breathless sything rush of air over tiny folded wings before the headlong dive is averted, and the bird flutters down to feed. At first they come singly, then in what sounds like larger wisps, until the air is filled with the sound of their coming. Just now and then a glimpse may be seen, but in the main they remain invisible. It is a joyous time, so that even when all of the light has long gone I am loathe to move for the snipe still come. They come in what sounds like hundreds, although it is no doubt substantially less, all rushing in some drawn out cavalcade of hungry little birds to get into the slush to probe 'with long straight bill . . . to fill its tiny gut'.

It is easy, even in the blindness caused by night's dark hand, to imagine the wild charge; to visualise the seering dive, and the last minute flutter as the landing site is selected. Alternatively the bird might move on a few feet before actually landing, but this is the work of but a moment. I sit there quietly, with the first chill of night visible in the vapourising of my breath, and consider the phenomenon. Yesterday I had been in this same spot, but there had been no snipe. Why had they chosen to come this day, rather than yesterday? Strangely, in all probability, there would be none on the morrow, though why this should be I could not say. This is one of the mysteries of bird behaviour, and goes a long way towards explaining why the wildfowler finds the quarry so fascinating. Were this not the case a great deal of the magic of the shore would disappear, and perhaps the wildfowler's devotion would also wane; fortunately the birds will never be fully understood, and in all honesty few would want it any other way.

I had shot a single snipe in that first crazy rush, before the light had all gone, with the only shot fired after the killing of the shoveler. The dog had brought it to hand and I had marvelled at its sporting qualities: ounce for ounce there can be few birds to rival the common snipe in terms of sporting value. The retrieving of a snipe is often amusing, for the tiny body will be almost invisible inside that cavernous mouth, with maybe no more than the bill and legs protruding. That bird was almost unmarked, save for a small spot of dark mud where it had fallen onto the salting, and was faintly moist from the warm interior of the canine mouth. When I eventually stood up those snipe that had landed close by made off with sharp calls of alarm, as did many others of their kind as I made my way back through the night. That night I swear the whole salting was full of snipe, the like of which I have not seen since – one man alone on the shore with another irreplaceable memory etched in the brain.

A moonlit December morning

The moon has a profound effect on the behaviour of wildfowl, as I shall outline later and, as a result, also on the hunting methods of us wildfowlers. As with any variation to a given norm there will be benefits, and often plenty on the debit side as well, but this is only to be expected and accepted. Thus the moon will be inclined to improve or spoil sport, dependant of course on circumstances. One example of moonlight ruining sport with great dependability, in my experience, is when the moon is on the wane, and thus still remains bright in the sky at morning flight. Invariably this will have the effect of lighting up the whole countryside like day and the great bulk of night-feeding ducks seem to use this as a good excuse to clear off to their roosts long before dawn – the net result being plenty of frustrated wildfowlers.

The season of which I write was a strange affair of occasional flurries of good sport, interspersed by long spells when there was precious little about. Even the normally reliable teal had not come to the saltings in any numbers, and it was a case of really scratching about for a bird or two, and this at what was normally one of the best periods of the whole season. Even though it flew in the face of all that I had learnt, I opted to try a morning flight at a time when I knew full well that the moon would be high in the sky before dawn. But desperation can be a strange bedfellow, and in theory anything is worth a try. This, allied to the highly fickle nature of wildfowl, led me to convince myself that I should remain optimistic. This was how I came to be parked beside the seawall well before dawn on a bright moonlit early December morn.

I changed into my wildfowling gear in unhurried fashion, for I was early and there was plenty of time. The tide was in a state of ebb, and as a result the whole shore was awash with bird noise as the multitude worked along the edge of the rippling water. From the top of the seawall I could just make out the edge of the saltings, whilst far away the moon played down upon the sea and just occasionally brought a sparkle of light to the eye. The ebb is one of the noisiest times on the shore, and on this morning it seemed noisier than ever. The gulls were kicking up a fearful din with constant raucous squawking, and one often wonders what all the fuss can be about; but they seem naturally argumentative and aggressive birds and, as with any possessing such temperament, will normally have a set-to at the slightest excuse! The ebb tide seems to be such an occasion. Of course a whole medley of birds can be heard at such a time: the tuneful piping redshank; the great sombre curlew; the sorrowful wail of the grey plover, but most strident of all the massed ranks of oystercatcher. On this morning the oystercatchers were really going to town in a big way, as though determined to drown out the vulgar gulls.

As I walked off to the west the main gull and wader roost fell behind, so that eventually the noise served as nothing more than a background. Ahead, where the shooting grounds lay, the shore was a good deal more orderly, with a few waders engaged in excited twittering conversation whilst plenty of quacking and whistling told me that already plenty of duck had gone out to roost. The morning flight was probably going to be as useless as all the signs indicated. Yet the morning was destined to provide another cherished memory, and if the same could be said for every flight, life would be most interesting indeed.

After a few minutes walking another sound joined with the medley of voices from the tideline; a sound half heard, half imagined; a sound to pluck at the memory chords, and set tiny prickles of excitement racing up the spine as old recollections swam into focus. Again, much closer this time, the lonesome yodel of geese – the high-pitched double note of the European white-fronted goose. I stood spellbound as they swept overhead, 17 of them in a ragged 'V' formation, bearing down from out of the north-east upon the tideway so near at hand; they called only spasmodically, instead of the intense and gossipy conversation so commonly associated with this species, and I suddenly felt a deep affinity for these most magnificent of birds. Soon I could hear them no more, so concluded that they had glided down onto the tide. Their presence at once delighted and intrigued me, for they were the first white-fronts that I had seen or heard that season; surely, I reasoned, these birds had just arrived on migration, and if so that would explain their quiet, almost weary, arrival on the shore.

When I squelched out across the newly washed salting the geese were there right enough, somewhere out on the edge. If they were in fact tired after a long journey they were not so weary as to lose their natural caution, for they soon became aware of my presence and made off along the coast; once again they were not very vocal, and I am still convinced to this day that they were indeed new arrivals. Yes, in common with so many of their brethren, they had come down on that glowing moon; they had seen the gently beckoning sheen of the tide below, and had murmured gratefully at the welcoming sight. The presence of one wildfowler had caused them no more than a passing inconvenience, so that they had done no more than move on a little out of harm's way.

It was a curiously wonderful and moving thing to witness the arrival of these birds; to know that no other English eyes had touched upon them since their last visit months before, and that in the between times they had travelled truly prodigious distances to and from their northern breeding grounds. I had seen them at one of their most secret and vulnerable moments, as they swept down to an English estuary on travel-weary wings. Soon others would know of their coming. Ornithologists would peer at them through myriad lens; other wildfowlers would hurry to the shore in hopeful anticipation, to try time without number to secure one of these fine birds for the pot. But for now I felt a certain pride; for just a while they were my geese – mine alone.

December teal

A few days later a friend and I went right off into the heart of the great saltmarsh in pursuit of the teal yet again. Tony was a good friend, but has long since left these parts, and has even forsaken the sport I believe. We had many good times together, and I shall long cherish the memory of him for, even if this sport be primarily a lonesome one, it is still pleasant to have one or two like-minded friends with whom one can share those special moments. On the drive down we had spotted some white-fronts feeding in the freshmarsh, and we sat a while and watched them from a knoll of high ground. Even though there were about 50 birds in the feeding flock I could not help but wonder if my 17 were amongst them; it was an exciting moment, and caused us to hurry to the shore with more than the usual quota of anticipation.

It was a normal enough sort of afternoon, and if the sky did not quite emanate that frost-laden feeling the air was certainly clear and bracing. It was a good sky for the evening flight, with one or two wisps of cloud and the slightest hint of a breeze, so that all that was needed were a few duck. A frustrating business this, the perpetual quest for those fickle teal flocks, made doubly difficult by the knowledge that though they may remain largely absent for long periods, all of a sudden they may arrive for no easily fathomable reason – rather similar in manner to the coming of the snipe I described earlier. This day as I stumbled through the saltmarsh I was in the grip of some undefinable excitement; the day seemed normal enough, and there were no birds about to generate such a feeling – but nevertheless it persisted.

Eventually I sat resting on the edge of a tiny mound of mud in that mucky part of the salting so beloved by snipe and the teal, and tried to reconcile the bursting anticipation within me. Perhaps its foundation lay in the sighting of the geese way back beyond the seawall, or in the knowledge that henceforth these great birds might decide to cross the salting without any warning. But I knew better than to believe any such basis existed. The 'feel' of which I wrote earlier was in the air. It invaded my being completely so that it was as strong as I can ever remember it, and a clear recognition of this fact served to heighten my excitement still further. Yes, I thought, with a tinge of satisfaction, this afternoon the teal would come. An intense longing consumed me as I waited, willing the birds to come and thereby confirm my faith in this sixth sense. I wondered if Tony too had detected this same feeling, but in later conversation it transpired that he had not. Poor Tony.

With the sun barely below the horizon I watched a single teal career across the saltmarsh, and a moment later heard the double shot as Tony missed and sent the bird in my direction. I crouched low over the dog and as the little bird came up to my left shoulder I sat up and killed it stone dead with a single shot. Most shooting men take a great delight in recording a kill on a bird already missed by a friend; this 'eye-wipe' is one of the supreme pleasures of the sport, and I too enjoy it immensely. If Tony had missed the spectacle I would be certain to remind him of the fact once flight was over. Having made this comment, I must confess to a considerable lack of interest in such matters when the boot is on the other foot! Another single teal caught me in this smug reflective mood, so that it evaded my first shot with speed and the second by the steepness of its climb as it lit the afterburners and punched upward in usual spectacular fashion. In a moment it would be out of range and heading in the direction of a doubtless vengeful Tony – probably harbouring ambitions of returning that eye-wipe – but I managed to clip it down with a broken wing. The bird, a plump little hen, dropped way off in the slushes and led the dog a merry old chase before she brought it back absolutely smothered in mud. Another teal came straight into the salting further away without a hint of hesitation, landing on the edge of the sea aster zone. Even though the light was still quite good it was an easy matter to stalk it, flush it at no more than 30 yards range and kill it as it made off. Thus a good beginning and, with the evening flight proper yet to begin, there was every sign that the 'feel' had indeed been genuine.

Was the atmosphere somehow charged, as if by an electric storm, in advance of the big teal flight? It was, of course, not possible to say, and maybe it was nothing more than a fanciful notion on my part. Yet the massed flight of the teal is like a feathered storm breaking upon the saltmarsh with an incredible ferocity, such is their mad desire to get in to feed. Once started, the flight will not be denied, with pack upon pack of tiny birds throwing themselves upon the saltings, mostly oblivious to gunfire which may be going on all around. So I shall try and describe those subsequent events through the eyes of the gunner, and in this way better relate the experience. Yet it is a difficult thing to achieve with mere words alone, without the celluloid aids of sound and the moving picture, and perhaps it will prove impossible to paint an accurate enough word picture for those with no knowledge of the phenomenon; such is a writer's lot, and I shall do my best.

So sit with me in the salting and peer into the ever-gathering gloom for any sign of their coming. The gun is cradled lightly upon the lap, gripped firmly yet in a relaxed and easy manner, ready to be raised and brought into action in a thrice: this is an important and easily overlooked aspect of shooting, for any excessive tension, if transmitted via your weapon, will be bound to result in a loss of shooting form. Difficult though it may often be, one must try and shoot in a relaxed and unhurried manner, for this will ultimately pay dividends in the shape of more accurate shooting. Ears strain to catch the tiniest sound, and as the gloom accelerates it is the ears that play an increasingly important role in providing first warning of any incomers. Then, quite suddenly, a bird is approaching; no need to call or even move as it comes past the left hand at a comfortable range and barely above the marsh. Swiftly and smoothly the gun is raised, the muzzle moves ahead of the speeding target and with a crash it is sent plummetting into the ground as a tiny broken bundle.

The swift pitter-patter, pitter-patter as the dog hurries to collect the fallen bird, and the spent cartridge is replaced quickly in case more come. Gunner and dog admire the bird, but for only the briefest of moments before once again concentrating on the sky in front. Again the single bird, although this one attempts to land out of range before the seductive call urges it to move on those few extra fateful yards which may mean the difference between life and death. On this day an extra 10 yards meant death for a hungry teal, and even as the bird falls the dog is away in a flash. This time she is slow in returning. Perhaps the bird is a runner, for the moment it is not possible to say, because the attention is diverted as a sound akin to the tearing of a huge sheet of cardboard rends the air, and a moment later a great pack of birds appears from the gloom. Now is the time to remain calm and pick a bird, even though this will be no easy matter for they are in at point-blank range and moving fast.

The effect of the shot is truly electric, for as a bird falls, the pack explodes upwards on furiously whirring wings. Again the gun fires, and again, but the speed of their flight carries them to safety, and the night sky soon hides them anyway. Suddenly the air seems full of birds as those that have sneaked in unseen fly off in alarm at the sudden spate of shooting, whilst the dog stands and stares at her dimly-seen master before continuing her search. The sound of tearing cardboard now fills the air as pack upon pack pour in. Some are mere spirits in the night, whilst others pass by just beyond the sensible range of the gun; yet others come right on in before seeing the dog perhaps and begin to turn quickly away, though not before the gun has claimed one of their number. Now the dog comes with a bird, a strong runner, and it is quickly taken and despatched with aplomb. 'Good girl'. I ruffle her neck, before urging her out again. 'Get on! Get on!'

The air is alive with rushing wings and hurtling black shapes and teal and yet more teal pour in. More shots at the swirling packs before the frantic fumbling for fresh cartridges is interrupted by a great mass of some 20 birds that burst either side of the wildfowler as he fires again to cause a bird to come spinning down. The dog has another bird, quite dead this time, but again I send her out to continue the pick up. The light is very bad now, though scarcely bad enough to hide the single mallard, a very slow and easy target after all those teal, which falls with a loud whack somewhere back in the salting, for the dog to retrieve it later.

Now there is a little time to think, for only the glow in the west provides light enough to shoot by, so that it is possible to disregard all else which is going on round about. The dog still snuffles her eager way through the slushes, diligently working to pick every bird; the bundle of tiny bodies lies nearby. At last, at last the teal have come. Still the air is filled with the rush of teal late for their banquet, hurrying past in the night, or occasionally landing close by in a flurry of pinions. It is a canopy of sound which seems to be endless, with only the movements of the dog intruding on the magic of the moment. Just now and again the odd bird hurtles across the western sky, but their speed saves them; only the odd bird slowing down to land will be likely to prove a realistic chance, and this would require more than a little luck. The whisper of wings from the void above causes the eyes to be raised, more out of habit than through any real sense of anticipation, and surprisingly the dim form of three birds at a reasonable height can be made out.

The wildfowler who has just got into a big teal flight, and done fairly well into the bargain, is a man flushed with success, and as such he will try anything. So it was this day and the gun was thrown up without a hint of hesitation, and the shot fired in one fluid movement; just time to see one of the birds fold up and then the darkness swallowed them. Then the wait, for what seems like an eternity, before what turns out to be the penultimate bird of the evening crashes onto the saltings. The dog brings this last bird – a magnificent drake pintail – and together man and animal sit in silence, basking in this glorious moment. Slowly the momentum of the flight begins to wind down, with fewer teal streaking past; then a sound, closer than most of the others, causes a new alertness – the eyes peer into that sliver of light low down in the west for the slightest glimpse.

The bird is seen for but a moment, but the senses are well honed, the reflexes razor sharp, and the crash of the gun knocks a bird down for the last time. The dog is away again, and this time there will surely be no more. The wildfowler smiles. No more than occasional racing birds can now be heard, and this is a time for speculation. Are these later birds hurrying to catch those that preceded them? If so then they are the fortunate ones, for the darkness now hides them so that they can flight with impunity, and the light is now too bad for their wild progress to be rudely arrested by man. Yes, the wildfowler is supremely happy. His faith and persistence and hard work have had just reward. Even when it is mostly quiet again he will sit and stare at the west, even though the light has all gone.

A sound from the east: Tony is coming. 'How many then?' The darkness hides the smile, '10 when the dog picks this one'. In another moment she has done so. The dog and the gun have worked well together; she has picked every bird, whilst the gun has hit almost 50 per cent of those speeding targets. Thus the flight was ended, and we left those teal which remained to quietly feed the night through inside the saltmarsh.

Here lies a salutory lesson for any wildfowler who finds himself stricken with a run of bad luck: invariably if he shows fortitude and persists in doing the things which he knows full well are right, the luck will change, and thus success will be all the sweeter. To give up in black despair will certainly solve nothing, and can only lead to a long-term failure. The old adage – practise makes perfect – is often very close to the truth. Personally I do not especially strive for perfection, for if I did I should undoubtedly go through life thoroughly disappointed. Perhaps we should merely strive to find our own level, and be content with that, for nobody can be truly

perfect. However, I apologise for any pain caused, for I can think of one or two people who would be genuinely shocked at such tarnishment of their perfection!

—9—

The Flooded Marsh

WITHOUT DOUBT WILDFOWL are amongst the most successful groups of birds in the world. This huge group of birds, encompassing geese, ducks and swans, includes many species and totals many millions of individuals; indeed, if we were to go further and use the American term 'waterfowl', then we could add yet more millions to this tally. Why are they successful? Why are they present in such huge concentrations? Difficult questions to answer fully perhaps, and in any case such deep deliberations scarcely have a place in this book; suffice to say that these birds have occupied an available niche, and it is a niche of great fertility and super abundance, which is obviously more than capable of sustaining such vast population densities.

Wildfowl are intensely gregarious. This is a fact which even the most inept of biologists will be quick to note, and logically they have evolved in such a way quite simply because this is the right thing for the particular species and, rather than being a matter of convenience, is no doubt a crucial part of their survival techniques. Doubtlessly there are good reasons for such a gregarious lifestyle, with self-defence high on the list. Even though most species have a diet which we could call semi-specialised, they are still fairly catholic in their tastes, and are therefore able to take advantage of seasonal variations in food availability. This is why such phenomena as the teal flight, described in the last chapter, occur, one moment not a bird to be seen, whilst maybe the very next day there can be a great concourse of birds within a relatively small area.

Of course the wildfowler understands all this, and even though the successful pursuance of his sport may at times seem a difficult thing to achieve, there will be plenty of occasions when he will enjoy good sport because wildfowl so relish the company of others of their kind. In this way a long standing, tried and trusted, defence mechanism can let them down; yet this is of no great long-term detriment, and the healthy state of all quarry species in terms of overall numbes testifies that this is so. Various hunting techniques have evolved over the years to take advantage of dense concentrations of wildfowl: clapnets, decoy pipes, punt-gunning, and even modern decoying and calling all use wildfowl habits to assist in bringing birds into the bag. In those days when such methods were used by professional wildfowlers, huge numbers of birds were taken; in comparison today's wildfowler takes an exceedingly modest cull of what is, after all, an amazingly abundant resource, with ample scientific evidence available to support this standpoint.

Decoying tactics
As I have already said, the use of decoying tactics in the flooded saltmarsh during the high tide period can provide some of the finest wildfowling sport available; nonetheless, it is to some extent a specialised form of the sport, requiring a good deal of preparation for what may be an outing of eight or nine hours duration. During the early part of the season, before the weather begins to turn really cold, such preparations need not be greatly concerned with aids to personal well-being and survival – always provided, of course, that one has taken adequate precautions with respect to tide and wind. Really any pre-trip planning will be confined to assessing the likeliest flighting places and the preparation of hide, decoys and calls, although once a routine for this type of sport has been established, few further problems should occur.

Although the temptation to take along everything including the kitchen sink may be considerable, in real terms convenience will be the determining factor. Weight and bulk must be given every consideration, especially as most such flighting places can only be reached after a long and frequently arduous trip across mud and saltmarsh; in real terms this will mean taking along the bare essentials and nothing more, so that any superfluous items must be left behind – unless one possesses the constitution of an ox. A wildfowler very soon learns that his quarry is used to a largely flat coast, and will therefore be intensely wary of an object which is too ostentatious. Of course exceptions to this rule do occur, with any permanent hides often happily accepted by the birds, and often these will not be associated with danger even if they are quite substantial structures. However, anything new which happens to stand above ground level will usually be given a wide berth, with only the odd foolhardy bird likely to be duped.

Thus the wildfowler intent on decoying birds at high tide is immediately presented with the problem of hiding from the sharp-eyed quarry, but at the same time doing so in as discreet a manner as he possibly can. Therefore, it follows that any hide must be as low to the ground as possible, whilst also blending in with the surroundings. Many wildfowlers will use flimsy bamboo-type canes as hide supports, with some form of camouflage netting to create a box-like structure inside which man and dog can hide. The majority of shop-bought camouflage netting will prove too dark by far for the browning winter saltmarsh, and in consequence will stick out like a sore thumb as a dark blotch on the marsh. In response to this, the thinking wildfowler will stain his hide to match the potential surroundings, and this will prove to be a thoroughly worthwhile exercise and in all probability will be worth a great number of extra birds in the bag over the course of the season. It is a very common practice to use such vegetation as can be found on site to enhance the appearance of the hide and to assist the blending in process. This is a perfectly acceptable practice so long as the delicate nature of some saltmarsh areas is taken into account, for it would be all too easy to cause irreparable harm to some fragile places such as exposed islands.

The result of substantial erosion.

In many of the south and east estuaries the complex saltmarsh system is mostly a by-product of such human activities as digging for clay. This has produced many islands and sheer-sided saltmarsh blocks which will often prove quite excellent sporting areas, with the food and shelter thus created almost irresistable to wild duck. Many such islands will be underwater around high tide, either partly or wholly dependant on the height of the tide, whilst at low water they will appear as towering clay banks topped by a tenuous scalp of greenery. These clay banks are easy prey to such erosive agents as stormy seas and severe frosts, both of which will cause the banks to crack and crumble away; additionally any unthinking act by Man may accelerate this relentless erosion, and is therefore to be avoided like the plague.

In some areas erosion is negligible, whilst in others – even within the same estuary – the damage may be severe, so that in time the total destruction of saltmarsh can take place. Any wildfowler worthy of the name must be aware of this likelihood and take the utmost care when hide building around the edges of such clay banks; in particular the uprooting of vegetation to aid hide building must be avoided, unless this takes place well back from the saltmarsh edge. Similarly any digging or such like should be avoided where it might cause accelerated erosion. Really common-sense should be applied, although some clubs which control the shooting rights over such land are not slow in making their members aware of the situation.

Accretion – that is the build-up of saltmarsh, via sedimentation and subsequent plant colonisation – can create saltmarsh, once again with this often occuring in an estuary where erosion is also taking place. However, there seldom seems to be a worthwhile exchange, as such accretion invariably consists of dense stands of *spartina* and so provides limited food for wildfowl and will destroy much valuable wader habitat on the open muds.

Having built the hide as close to the water's edge as is practical it only remains to set the decoy pattern, await the flood tide and, with good fortune, enjoy some sport. However, as with all good things in life, setting an effective decoy pattern is not quite as easily accomplished as might be imagined. One of the most common errors committed by the inexperienced will be the incorrect siting of the decoy pattern. It must always be remembered that decoys set up during the low tide period may well look ideally placed, but come the flood tide the wildfowler may find himself forced back further than anticipated with the end result being that the decoys will be situated on the very limit of range. This defeats the whole object of a decoying exercise, which is to bring birds within a comfortable killing range, and as such should encourage deeper consideration before final setting up.

When decoying, whatever the potential quarry, I always set my pattern fairly close in – in the 20–30 yard bracket at a maximum – so that any target will receive the full benefit of the shot pattern. Additionally one must always bear in mind that many birds are prone to pitch in short of the decoys, so that a close-set pattern should still allow a few shots at these more reluctant birds. On occasions birds will be a little decoy-shy so that any pattern set on the limit of range will probably mean little, if any, sport, as the quarry either shies away or drops in out of range. One method commonly used to counter any reluctance on the part of the birds will be to increase the size of the decoy 'flock'. Generally this will be limited by the wildfowlers' carrying capacity, but with modern-day lightweight decoys, bulk rather than weight will prove the determining factor. Nevertheless it is possible to carry 20 or more decoys, and such a 'flock' can prove a substantial attraction to any passing birds. Many will have seen pictures of North American decoying tactics involving huge numbers of artificials. Transposed into an English situation this sort of tactic would be taking things to an extreme, but in the USA this is obviously worthwhile – else our trans-Atlantic cousins would scarcely go to so much bother.

An estuary – even a fairly small one – is a large place, and at high tide there will be an awful lot of water for any wandering pack of birds to choose from. It will therefore be essential to correctly assess where the birds are most likely to be, and thereafter be able to take advantage of the situation. A flooded creek packed with decoys can often yield a substantial return in terms of sporting opportunity, and thus provide ample recompense for the inevitable labour involved. However, the reader must guard against using the maximum number of decoys on every occasion; although this will prove of benefit in the majority of instances, there are many times when a lot less effort can produce a surprisingly good result. Mostly the experienced wildfowler will know when to scale down his operation, with trial and error usually the basis for future success.

There will be times when a simple pair of decoys deposited into some salting pool or in some grubby creek bottom, will work wonders, especially if accompanied by astute calling. Equally there are many instances where the use of any decoys at all will prove a total waste of time. Obviously such times will not always be immediately discernible, but, as with all facets of the sport, it will

Fitting a light weight to hold the decoys in a non-tidal situation.

eventually be possible to narrow down percentages to a point where the experienced man can mostly get it right.

The actual setting of decoys needs to be done in an efficient manner if one or two embarrassing pitfalls are to be avoided. Many places which prove ideal for decoying are subject to a fair degree of tidal flow, so logically decoys will need to be anchored effectively; for this the use of weights is a common practice, although short stakes pushed into the mud are equally useful. If using weights – whether lead or iron – it will be advisable to keep these to a minimum for obvious reasons. Rather than anchor decoys individually, in which case a great number of weights will be required, it will prove more viable to join them together in teams of four or six lying astern; some even favour a long stream of a dozen or more decoys held by a common anchor, and there is nothing wrong with this method so long as the anchor is reliable. There is nothing worse than seeing an expensive collection of decoys disappearing out to sea on the ebb tide.

Weights need not be excessive in the majority of cases, with something in the order of 4 oz pushed into the mud normally more than adequate. Wooden stakes, if preferred, should also be pushed firmly into place, with anchor strings tied securely. My preference is for small weights, but I do use stakes where the tidal flow is likely to be severe. I also prefer smaller groups of decoys over long streams although there is scarcely any logical reason for such a bias. Modern monofilament fishing line, of a reasonably high breaking strain in the order of 15lb, is my choice for both anchor lines and shorter lines connecting decoys. The big advantage associated with these heavier lines is their greater reluctance to tangle, so that setting up can be accomplished with the minimum of delay. Obviously the anchor lines will need to be of sufficient length to cope with the height of tide, otherwise the red-faced wildfowler might find his first one or two 'birds' underwater! Lines connecting additional decoys need to be no more than two or three feet in length to present a realistic picture.

Actual retrieval will usually present few problems, for most tide-flighting wildfowlers will set their decoy pattern at low water and pick up after the ebb-tide; in practice this will present few problems, as mostly it will not be possible to get away from the marsh earlier anyway. Where there is a need to recover the decoys whilst they are still afloat, various methods must be devised to achieve this. A long line attached to the pattern, by which they can be dragged in at any time, is much favoured, although this can present practical problems; alternatively a free line, with weight attached, can be cast over floating decoys and used to haul the whole lot in. This latter method is my favourite where decoys are set close-in, but wildfowlers are nothing if not inventive, and can be relied upon to come up with diverse ways of achieving a common goal.

Calling

Calling wild duck – that is imitating the call of the particular species and thereby attempting to attract it within shooting range – is a skill in itself and can be highly effective at times. If used correctly, in conjunction with a good spread of decoys, it can often be an excellent way of swelling the bag. Many artificial calls are available, some of which are very good – only experience will help to differentiate the good from the bad, although it undoubtedly pays to treat such items of equipment with a degree of caution. Sometimes it is possible to spot a raw recruit to the sport by the miscellany of calls draped about his person. Such newcomers should tread with great care if they are not to earn an unenviable reputation, for nothing rankles more than a constant discordant barrage of calls from the saltmarsh – most of which will probably have the opposite effect to that intended. Even the best of calls will only work well if used correctly, so a degree of proficiency will be an early aim.

My point about long periods spent in apparently slothful contemplation of the surroundings becomes forcefully rammed home when one considers that it is at such times that the observant wildfowler will learn much about his quarry. If he notes both movement and sound he will quickly come to understand something of duck language, and such knowledge will become invaluable later on. By all means purchase and use artificial calls, even though their use is fraught with problems. The muddy conditions of the foreshore will be bound to take a toll of all wildfowling 'impedimenta', and calls are certainly no exception; indeed they are highly susceptible to loss, damage or blockage, usually at the most inconvenient of times. Even when suspended from a lanyard around the neck they may not remain impervious to foreshore conditions.

Without question the wildfowler's own voice will provide the most effective, durable and long-lasting of all calls, although the trick of learning to quack, whistle and the like may not be accomplished in a moment. Plenty of practice, preferably at the local park or bird collection rather than on the marsh, will be necessary, whilst a fairly thick skin in anticipation of the inevitable leg-pulling will also be a useful aid to perfecting this art. By good observation, the wildfowler can learn to mimic those softer murmurings, so common amongst the birds at those quiet secretive times when few people will be abroad to hear them. Often it is the tiniest of nasal 'kneaps' which will prove deadly, and this should be remembered at all times. To be able to attract wild birds by the use of one's own voice is an attribute held with some pride by those who have mastered it, and rightly so, for there can be few greater satisfactions than calling up a distant bird and summarily adding it to the bag with the sweetest of shots. Obviously some species will be easier to call than others, whilst some people can master this art with ease whereas others might practice for a lifetime without achieving satisfactory results.

My advice is to learn how to call and, of equal importance, when to call and when to remain silent, and in this way one can greatly increase the likelihood of coming away from the shore with a bird or two. Above all ignore the ragging of your peers, many of whom really should know better. As will be seen from the pages of this book, I am a self-taught caller of wildfowl, and know that because of this ability I am going to add many birds to my bag which might otherwise have passed safely beyond the limits of range. This ability was not in-built, but came as a direct result of the observation and the practice I have advocated over the last few chapters. Many examples of successful calling come readily to mind, but one perhaps stands out as a grandstand spectacular before a full house.

The occasion was an invited evening flight on a delightful marsh which lies near the River Thames in Kent. It was a tame, early season day, and an absolute joy to be out in the open air – although scarcely the sort of weather to inspire dreams of great wildfowling deeds. Amongst the small assembly was a good-natured gamekeeper-type whose great joy on such days was to rag me at every opportunity. He teased me for using a pump-action shotgun, for making 'funny little squeaks' at flight, and most of all for writing the odd word on my chosen sport. He splashed off into the adjacent hide, so that all I could see was the top of his hat and, though I tried hard, I could not imagine it as a fat duck!

It was still well light – a time to sit in idle contemplation of the surroundings and think of the many good days which I had enjoyed over the years. After a good while a solitary teal crossed the marsh a long way off, heading purposefully elsewhere and

obviously totally oblivious to our presence. A few 'funny little squeaks' later it had turned and was headed in our direction. Once the bird's attention had been taken it was time to keep quiet and let it come on, which it did without further hesitation. The little bird came as straight and as swift as an arrow, so that it merely remained for me to show myself and kill it as it began to climb away. It landed nicely between my tormentor and I, and significantly he said not a word. Lesson number one: Keep practising the calling. Lesson number two: Ignore foolish abuse from people who know no better.

Tide-flighting in the flooded estuary is undoubtedly a sphere of the sport requiring a good deal of wildfowling know-how and expertise if it is to be accomplished both successfully and safely. Perhaps not to be recommended to the outright beginner, but most definitely one of the most effective ways of filling the bag.

—10—

The Edge of the Tide

THE TRUE WILDFOWLER, that denizen of the open shore and creek-cut saltmarsh, is mostly obliged to remain at the behest of the greatest of all natural elements – the tide. For the movement of the tide governs the lives of all creatures of the shore, from the tiniest of micro-organisms to the most majestic of seabirds. Given this undeniable fact, the wildfowler must go where his quarry draws him, whilst it in turn is subjected to the overwhelming influence of the tide.

The tide can be many things to many creatures. To the wildfowler it can be the provider of sport, or it can quite ruin sport – dependent on circumstances. It can growl and menace, and thus warn off he who may be about to set foot on the shore, or it can be quiet and gentle and sneak in to kill the unwary. The tide will always be there, and will do as it will, regardless of Man's puny aspirations. Whether sport is provided or not, one can guarantee that the movement of the tide will present a rich table for the wildfowler/ornithologist to feast at. Often sport will not material-ise, but always there will be something to see so that few trips to the shore can be dismissed as a waste of time.

Few wildfowlers can fail to be astounded at the splendour of the grey geese which throng to the coast each winter, for they are as great a stimulation as could be found in any sport for any hunter. These mighty birds are less affected by the tide than many of their smaller cousins, although even they can scarcely remain totally oblivious to its moods. That true maritime goose, the small, noisy brent, is a different matter entirely, and its life is tied comprehensively to the movements of the tide, especially during the early part of the winter. Two separate races visit our shores each winter: the light-bellied brent, which is mainly confined to the north and Northern Ireland, and the dark-bellied brent which winters on the south and east coasts. It is this latter bird with which I am familiar, and all further references to the brent goose will mean this.

Brent geese

The brent now pile into our south and east estuaries in unprecedented numbers of anything up to 90,000 birds. For a protected species of wildfowl this is an awfully large number of birds, and in consequence the eyes of many sportsmen are turned in this direction; however the issue is beyond the scope of this book, and is a matter with which the BASC is ably dealing. I view the brent mainly from an aesthetic, even romantic, viewpoint. I am not old enough to have enjoyed the brent as a legal quarry – pre 1954 – and have never viewed it as anything other than an ornithologist's goose. To me it is part of the winter scene on the coast, and even if it is now too numerous in many ways I for one would not wish to be without it. Without doubt the brent has given me many hours of enjoyment, and hopefully I shall long view this species in such a light. Some of these moments are worth relating, and will thus hopefully convey something of their noisy exuberant character to the reader; if thereafter the reader craves for more, then I suggest that a November journey to one of the major estuaries or harbours will more than suffice! The brent is known as one of the black geese, a distinction which it shares with that gigantic aerial picnic hamper of a bird the Canada goose. There any common factor ends, for one could scarcely find two goose species with more contrasting habits; indeed few wildfowlers consider the Canada in the same breath as their grey quarry geese, or view it with the sort of endearment often reserved for the brent. When seen from a distance the brent will certainly seem an almost totally black bird, but upon closer examination a different image emerges. Indeed there is much black, although this will be complemented by dark greys and browns on the back, underside and wings. There will be white too, albeit in small quantities, but enough to present a quite startling contrast with that ultra-dark body. All brent sport that typical goose half moon of white above the tail, whilst the adults also have white neck markings. These neck markings serve as an invaluable aid to wildfowl counters, making it possible to assess the annual percentage of young birds with the minimum of effort, and thereafter to reach a swift appraisal of breeding success.

Being a goose does not automatically qualify a species for great size, for in the hand the brent is scarcely any larger than a sheldrake. However, in the wild its long broad wings and dark colouration help to give an impression of considerable size; its posture is erect and proud, in typical goose fashion, and its powerful wings will soon carry it out of harm's way. The voice is highly distinctive; a low shortened growl almost, which will become, in the company of many others in a large flock, a concerted cacophony of sound, perhaps reminiscent of a swarm of raucous angry bees. Whether the low, contented murmur of the feeding flock, or the more strident tones of that flock when en route to or from the feeding grounds, the voice of the brent is like that of no other coastal bird.

The feeding pattern of the brent is fairly well defined and as a result anyone who knows this pattern can enjoy some spectacular brent-watching sessions. Early season they will graze avidly on both *zostera* and algae; during the high tide period they will retire to some safe roost, either on the water or on the higher saltmarsh. Large numbers of hungry brent will soon decimate the food supply of the mud flats, with a natural progression taking them to new grazing areas on the mature saltmarsh. Soon enough they will be raiding inland, in the manner of grey geese, feeding on pasture, cereal and even rape. With the increase in numbers the flocks now move to the inland fields earlier than ever before, thus heightening the inevitable conflict with agricultural interests.

There are various methods suitable for real close-range study of brent, and these may come about as a useful spin-off from wildfowling rather than from some deliberate ploy aimed at the brent itself. When in pursuit of the often elusive wigeon, the brent can be observed from the crude shelter afforded by some filthy hole dug into the *zostera* beds. Sometimes the geese will stay in the same area for long periods, but more often they will be gently on the move in solid lines of eagerly grazing birds – a ripple of darkly

These brent are soon raiding inland in great flocks.

coloured birds moving over the sombre greys of the mud. Perhaps the best method of securing abundant sightings is to wait in some shallow creek out on the edge of the saltmarsh as the tide begins to flood. Then, as the tide covers more and more mud, the brent will begin to flight past in small and large skeins, flying low over the waves and calling in that excited buzzing manner. Generally they will fly right off down the shoreline to a favourite roost, but if one is really lucky some may pitch into the water close by. Once this occurs other parties soon join the roosting flocks until a great mass of birds may be congregated, floating contentedly on the tide. If the wildfowler waits patiently in his creek until the muddy brown water comes scudding through and the tide is rippling all about his position, he may find geese all around him.

Whether as a direct result of some disturbance or because of nothing more than a quirk of behaviour, I do not know, but on occasion the geese will come in one great noisy mass – so that they momentarily darken the sky low down above the tideway. Where they land close by there arises a great thrashing of wings and uplifting babble of voices, prior to a general settling down to a happy murmur.

Take a typical flood tide as viewed through the eyes of the waiting wildfowler. The tide has long since forced its first grubby finger past your position in the creek bed; already the water is knee-deep and rising with a remorseful finality, until the tide edge is only a few yards away – soon it will be time to quit the creek and head for drier parts. At first the sound is faint and elusive, indistinct in the gusting wind, before rising in crescendo until the birds burst into view around a bend in the shoreline. In a matter of moments there are 500 or 600 of them bearing down upon you half-hidden in the creek, the noise deafening and the sky thronging with birds. They begin to split up, breaking the ragged formation to turn over the shallows searching for a suitable place to land. Some head on down the tideline, whilst others swing right over the filling creek at barely 15 feet in height – a host of broad bellies and, as they turn, flashing white rumps.

They take little or no notice of the wildfowler, seemingly safe in the knowledge that he will do them no harm, instead insolently splashing into the shallows close by. Yet even though they exude a superficial nonchalance, the whole flock remains intensely alert, a forest of erect necks that they might better watch for any hint of danger. For a while their vocal tones remain subdued, but in an instant they see the wildfowler rise as if from the waves, and they in turn lift as one to distance themselves from this alarming spectre. It

Brent sweeping past low over the tideway.

is then, driven by a momentary panic, that the birds are at their most vocal, but the wind soon plays across their primaries to carry them on to some other place where they might while away the high tide period.

Later on in the season, when the brent flocks are grazing the higher saltmarshes, it is often possible to complete a perfect stalk, under fairly easy conditions, in order to get to within close spying range of the feeding mass. In those places where the saltmarsh falls away via steep clay banks it is not too difficult to creep by unseen, or alternatively stop off for some idle watching with this frequently, requiring nothing more energetic than stooping a little from the upright walking position. For such a stalk it is as well to imagine that the target flock in fact consists of grey geese, and that the ultimate objective is to obtain a worthwhile shot; in this way the wildfowler is likely to display more perseverance and determination, thus increasing the likelihood of success. Slowly the approach is made, with their voices becoming ever louder and serving to guide the stalker to their exact location. Slowly, lest they take fright, the wildfowler will peer above the clay bank and at last they are there – some 200 strong with the closest birds barely 40 yards away. Some will be feeding, many idly loafing, whilst still others stand sternly on guard duty – lest Man or some wandering raptor pose a superficial threat.

Their idyllic murmur tends to remind one of a concourse of simple folk engaged in idle gossip – if the brent were occupied in some similar pastime it is difficult to imagine a worthwhile topic for such intense conversation. Perhaps they are discussing the weather; or the choice of foodstuffs currently on their menu; perhaps it is future breeding prospects on the far-off northern coasts, or some retrospective discourse on their recent arduous southward migration. Yet in all probability none of these things concerns the brent except in the very moment of participation. The life of a brent goose is likely to be a good deal less complicated than that.

It is instantly obvious when they have spotted their observer, for momentarily the conversation becomes subdued as an almost telepathic alarm spreads through the flock. Then all heads are up and a new urgency fills the air, so that this time there can be no doubt about the topic of conversation. A brief moment of restlessness presages a mighty roar of wings and clamour of voices as they take to the air. It is an incredible sight as the great mass climb desperately away, with here and there a shelduck scattered amongst the host, rather akin to some giant swirling snowflakes against a backcloth of black stormy skies. A remarkable thing this panic-stricken uplifting of birds as they rise in a chain reaction ripple of thrashing wings and flashing white rumps. In no time at all they are turning with the wind some 90 yards away, before fleeing on the wings of that unseen force towards the safety of the sea.

More to watch than quarry
For the wildfowler who skulks patiently at the edge of the tide there will be plenty more to see besides his quarry and those super-abundant brent geese. Admittedly other creatures may prove a little less spectacular but they are no less a pleasure to watch, and in some instances their comparative scarcity multiplies their interest value. Note that tiny, short-tailed weasel which is apparently living in the stony crevices higher up the seawall, where only the very largest of spring tides can reach. On this occasion it is engaged in the half-hearted stalk of an alert pair of meadow pipits; the stalk is closely watched by the two, who eventually tire of being potential prey and flutter away to safer parts. Thus thwarted the tiny mammal returns to its warm shelter at breakneck speed. Soon it re-emerges. There can be no doubting that this is the original animal, for it sports a distinctive and rather unusual white spot on the tip of its nose. Once in the open it stops and scratches furiously at various parts of the body; thereafter it conducts a rudimentary search of some nearby vegetation, where it can only be hunting for

insects. If this be the aim then it achieves no more success than in the abortive pipit hunt.

The hunt is interrupted at frequent, if irregular intervals by that frantic dash back to the security of its hiding place. Here the tiny form will disappear, only to peep out again almost immediately in the most comical manner; then, after ascertaining that the coast is clear, it will once again venture forth. However, the actual hunt seems to be of no more than secondary importance to the serious business of mounting a succession of furious counterattacks against the rather over-zealous parasites which seem to inhabit the tight brown fur – which will be done by repeated and rapid scratching of the portion currently under attack. One is left to reflect upon the fact that whatever befalls this deadly little predator, it will never rid itself entirely of these parasites, and will thus remain destined to spend the remainder of its hectic life engaged in fruitless scratching. Such is a weasel's lot. In observing the weasel the fact comes to mind that the great majority of creatures on the coast are predators of a sort, even if one does not readily associate their activities as outright predation. But any creature which feeds on another organism – be it a fellow bird or mammal, or some ostensibly insignificant invertebrate – can be said to predate, so that it can be quickly discerned that the list is likely to be a long one.

Many birds of prey are present each winter on our coasts and, although the numbers of individual species will never be high, there can be no ignoring the interesting variety on offer. Variety is said to be the spice of life, and this is undoubtedly so in ornithological terms: thus to find harriers, a variety of owls, plus less common species such as buzzard, merlin and peregrine falcon all present on the same coastal plain is a spicy mixture indeed. Of all our coastal birds of prey without question the most common and ubiquitous is the kestrel. There can be few adults in these islands who could not recognise a kestrel without hesitation, for it can be seen almost anywhere that there is a rough corner capable of attracting some tiny mammal upon which the species will prey. It will be present on the coast because of the abundance of rough and untidy cover, and the consequential population of prey. It can be seen less commonly hunting the saltmarshes, but will frequent the densely grassed earthen seawalls with great regularity and will display a justified trust in any onlooker, thereby allowing some quite excellent sighting opportunities. It is so common as to scarcely warrant description but, for all that, it is a bird which occupies an important place at the edge of the tide.

The kestrel is a delightful mixture of beauty and grace combined with that ruthless killer instinct of all its kind. It must kill to survive, and it survives most successfully indeed; it is a merciless killer of those tiny rodents which cower in terror-filled lives beneath the seer winter grasses, but because of its form we can scarcely feel any revulsion for its gruesome lifestyle. Watch the swift, direct flight suddenly arrested by the glimpse of a movement below amongst the matted stems. Sometimes the bird will hover briefly before moving on; alternatively it may hover lower and ever lower, so that the onlooker will expect to witness a successful strike – then, at the crucial moment, it will lift and fly on.

The actual hover, which is the hunting technique of this distinctive species, is a remarkable phenomenon. Focus the binoculars and watch the bird closely and you will note that all wing and tail movements are with one object in mind: to keep the head, and therefore the eyes, steady so that it can take an accurate focus on any possible target below. It is remarkable how adept at this technique is the kestrel, for it is able to remain on an even keel in all but the strongest of winds. For the patient, and above all discreet, observer the sight of a successful kestrel strike will be well worth waiting for. Strange that it is so difficult to feel any compassion for a slaughtered vole or mouse, or some other unfortunate; but the kestrel is as fine a bird as ever felt the wind flooding past its primaries, whilst a vole is a secretative and largely unloved little fellow. Life goes on towards infinity on the coast, and only barbaric death can sustain it.

—11—

And So to the New Year

APART FROM SPARODIC periods of post-New Year hard weather conditions of frost and snow, the November/ December period ought to provide the most consistent sport of the entire season. All aspects of the sport described thus far can be at a zenith, plus some excellent moonlighting can be enjoyed on these two full moon periods. Any wildfowler will be well advised to make the most of this halcyon period while he can, for come the turn of the year the quality of sport invariably becomes worse.

The modern trend of an almost total shutdown of work for a period approaching two weeks from Christmas to New Year seems to produce something of a watershed in sporting terms on the shore; for most wildfowlers can get in a few trips to the shore, whilst almost every piece of land will be subject to some shooting pressure or other. The inevitable result will be a population of somewhat harassed wildfowl. Admittedly the ample bevy of coastal refuges scattered around the country helps to negate such an effect, but there is a fall-off in sport after this national beanfeast. Personally I avoid too much wildfowling during this period, for I greatly prefer it when the marshes are mostly devoid of fellow sportsmen so that I can enjoy the restful, unfettered pursuance of the sport – which is for many the initial attraction anyway.

Yet such is the perverse nature of the sport there are going to be some seasons when even during this peak period the birds will be elusive, and sport correspondingly much reduced. At such times it will be necessary to take advantage of any favourable turn of events – such as a sharp frost or a big wind – and hope that this will make the quarry a little more co-operative. Of course such a combination of ideal wildfowling weather and good sport does not necessarily materialise – to the inevitable chagrin and frustration of the wildfowler. In fact I know of many men who scarcely bother to venture out unless conditions are 'ideal' and, without doubt, they frequently rob themselves of much good sport; however, this is their loss, and the gain of those prepared to remain optimistic enough to persevere through the bad times. Admittedly there is nothing quite like a big flight in some raging gale, in terms of excitement, but for filling the bag there is much to be said for grubbing about amongst the saltings for the odd bird on those windless frosty nights.

I have lost count of the number of times I have gone to the shore when conditions were ostensibly hopeless. A clear, cloudless sky; a sharp hint of a frost to come, with not a bird to be seen anywhere. But on such still nights many duck may come whispering in at deepest dusk – albeit seldom in any great concentrations – and it will often be possible to make a bag. Such calm conditions are absolutely ideal for picking off these odd wandering birds, for they will often respond dramatically to some astute calling. Teal, mallard, wigeon and other less plentiful species all go to make for an interested and varied range of quarry to tempt the wildfowler to return time without number to these secret little creeks and mud pans.

December flighting
One afternoon, not long after the big influx of teal described in an earlier chapter, found me further down on the coast tucked into a dense stand of *spartina*. It was a useful vantage point, with a wide vista of the saltmarsh spreading away all around me; a wide creek lay to my west, and it was here that I hoped any birds would come, with teal obviously very high on the list of probable customers. Even with plenty of light remaining, the odd bird could be seen whispering its way towards the tempting inland marshes. A chill began to settle over the shore, so that soon I felt it tingling at my fingertips and plucking at the exposed flesh of cheeks and ear lobes. Yes, indeed, it would be a white one before the night was over.

A single large duck appeared off to the west, etched clearly against the burning aftermath of the sun, and headed across my front at an oblique angle. It responded to my call instantly, swinging in a wide arc to the north so that it eventually came down the very centre of the creek, and low enough to present few problems if I shot to form. But I badly misjudged the speed of the bird, so that the first shot missed well behind. Then the fleeing bird was soaring determinedly for the safety of the void above on wildly threshing wings, so that a renewed sense of urgency urged my swing on to greater accuracy for the killing second shot. Even so the shot was an untidy affair, for the bird fell in that manner so reminiscent of a wounded target: head up, feet flailing wildly, with perhaps a good wing flapping uncontrollably in a desperate attempt to stay airborne. Yet despite such valiant effort it sploshed into the mud some 30 yards away. Such a bird can present problems for even an experienced retriever if it should land in water, or a combination of water and semi-flooded salting, but on this occasion a surface of bare clinging mud could act as precious little comfort for a wounded bird with a dog swiftly approaching. The retrieve was duly accepted and my first female pintail of the season despatched and stowed away.

The pintail comes to these saltings infrequently, so it was even more surprising to find three more of these graceful birds swinging around the creek in expectant fashion at my gentle calling. Frustration took over as they made one cautious circuit before clearing off into the gathering gloom, to leave me ruefully reflecting on what might have been. One or two teal came hurtling past, but seemed to be heading purposefully for other parts; most certainly they took no notice of my oft-times magical teal call, and

Somber wintry afternoon.

141

left me to sit in contented possession of the pintail. Quite suddenly a pair of bottle-shaped black-looking wigeon plummetted out of the west heading for the apparently inviting goo of the creek. Shame on me for reaching a state of blissful daydreaming, so that from start to finish they had the advantage of me, with none of my three forlorn shots connecting. Thus the pleasure of the pintail was a little tarnished by this final act of ineptitude, and this was enough to give me some sobering food for thought on the return journey. Still it would scarcely do for us to achieve an excessively high success rate.

December fell away towards the New Year in the grip of some pretty severe frosts for the time of year. Unfortunately these were scarcely sharp enough to improve sporting prospects on the shore more than an iota, so I spent an awful lot of time shivering, with precious little actual shooting to make it a worthwhile exercise. There were, as always, plenty of wigeon in the area, but in the absence of any strong headwind the flocks were apt to flight very high indeed; occasionally they would be just within shooting range, but as high birds have never been my strong point anyway I found it difficult to hit the target with any sort of consistency. We wildfowling writers tend to largely disregard our blank flights, for they seldom make for spellbinding reading; but let me assure the reader that blanks there are, frequently in profusion, so let nobody run away with the impression that life is one never ending idyll of successful flights.

A cursory note in my diary concerning one such flight states in a masterpiece of understatement, 'I shot very badly again'! Behind this bland message lies a wealth of disaster and might have been, but strangely my pen found difficulty in recording too much detail; suffice to say that it was very windy, with the teal coming like bullets, and I picked up two birds for my 17 expended cartridges. Now who on earth would want to read a blow by blow account of such a débâcle? Still less fun to write of such an experience.

Canada geese

A good-natured friend invited me to an impromptu morning shoot in an old run-down quarry. He was enthusiastic about the considerable population of rabbits, whilst pigeons and the odd party of mallard sometimes put in an appearance. Yet the main reason for my acceptance was that the shoot was nicely situated on a well-used Canada goose flightline, and as I had not shot a Canada up to that time I was keen to put the record straight. Even though I have never viewed the Canada with any great affection, it can scarcely be denied that this largest of all our geese is well worth powder and shot, and is no worse when laid upon the dinner plate than any of its contemparies. Yet, for all that, this species is a naturalised import from North America; is very metropolitan in its lifestyle, and is a semi-wild, feral quarry rather than a full blown will 'o' the wisp member of the wildfowl tribe.

My host, who was no wildfowler even if he did possess aspirations in this direction, told me that he had been studying the movements of the geese, and that they could be relied upon to flight through at the same time each morning. Their time was not at the breaking of the day but later – at a somewhat more civilised hour. Thus it was with a mixture of horror and trepidation that I agreed to meet him at the appointed hour, with the sun already nudging above the horizon. I was in tetchy mood, for this was no way to approach the morning flight, but as a guest I was in no position to argue one way or another.

On arrival at the quarry gates we were greeted by the nightwatchman at the nearby building site. Now it transpired that the ambush masterplan had in fact evolved as a joint effort between my host and this ageing sage, so perhaps it was not too surprising to discover that things had gone wrong. The watchman told us that a skein of Canada geese, some 19 strong, had flown through less than 15 minutes before; they were both aghast, having never known such a thing before. This was enough to make any self-respecting wildfowler turn green at the gills, and my emotions swung between disappointment at having missed the skein and sheer amazement at their naïvety. After some discussion I waited on the flightline lest any more skeins should come through, whilst my host cheerfully set off in pursuit of a rabbit or two. Damn the rabbits! As for bungling, amateur wildfowlers, . . . !

There was not a breath of wind and the night had produced a hard frost, so the ground was frozen almost solid. It was bitterly cold, with the sun failing to make any impression at such an early hour. I stood close-in to a stand of hazel trees so that I should have a little cover if the unlikely happened and more geese came through, but it was a morning totally devoid of inspiration in the absence of the perpetual magic of the shore. To my right ran a long double line of trees, mostly willows, whilst between these fed a small stream. The occasional wood pigeon clattered to and from these trees, while within this sparse bower a trio of raucously squawking jays plied their despicable trade. Had they come near enough I should have vented my spite on this most attractive of all the crows, but even this shallow satisfaction was to be denied me.

The deep bass of a flying Canada drove any further thoughts of murdering jays from my mind, and brought a swift sharpening of the senses. A moment later I knew they were heading my way as the occasional single call betrayed their passage; then they were past and I had still not seen a feather, with the calls echoing back from the stream and the stoic willows. A few seconds later I saw nine of them rise from the willows some 150 yards away, to disappear on the far side as suddenly – the cursed birds had flown the length of the stream below treetop height and I was thus thwarted for the second time in one morning. That was it, and I stamped back to the car in a state of high dudgeon. A joyous host arrived with a single rabbit, and a sympathetic ear for my tale of woe: he promised me another try for the Canadas, and this time we would arrive at the first crack of the day. One day, Canada goose. One day . . . !

Christmas Eve
So the festive period lay just around the corner, with a brief final foray to the shops early on Christmas Eve fulfilling my sense of duty on such matters. This done I was free to try a flight before the holiday rush began. I know of many who scorn such an unfestive act as Christmas Eve wildfowling, but I see it as an almost sure way of having the shore to oneself, whilst one's fellows will be grudgingly tramping around the countryside delivering presents and other festive fare. At such times it pays to finish these chores a day or two earlier, even if it be a selfishly motivated act. I can think of few greater pleasures in life than being alone on a flooded saltmarsh, with only a dog and a few wild birds for company, whilst the rest of the nation is in an hysterical turmoil of goodwill to all men. Such is pleasure to a dedicated wildfowler, although I can appreciate this being viewed as an odd-ball activity by the great majority.

I found myself an ideal inner curve within the centre of a favourite island, so that the wind was just right for both decoying and the retrieval of any shot birds which chanced to fall a long way out in the tide. I built a low hide out of a mixture of discarded wood, long grasses and sea purslane taken from the centre of a wide piece of salting, being mindful of the height of the last tide – clearly discernible by a scruffy mark of abandoned debris. As it turned out I judged this to perfection, for the tide flooded the hide with no more than a bare inch of mucky water at its height. The flood tide coincided with dusk, providing me with one of my favourite wildfowling circumstances, and throughout the after-noon, as the tide made, I was able to sit back and await events with a

Deep creek at low tide.

sense of ever-heightening anticipation. Curious how the tide can push into these salting areas, flooding the creeks and mud pans, before sneaking in amongst the vegetation largely unnoticed; then all of a sudden the whole area will be awash, save for the stems of sea aster protruding as desultory reminders of the salting's former glory.

A dozen decoys rode innocently at anchor barely 20 yards in front of the hide, and as the light began to fade a tranquil feeling settled over me. A little way off a few brent had drifted in, and they now came into the shallows to spend the last of the light greedily up-ending for algae and other juicy titbits; shelducks were scattered like giant blocks of polystyrene on the rippling floods and the odd trip of dunlin flipped past heading who knows where. Four teal skirted the tide, before passing some 40 yards out, seemingly uninterested in the decoy pattern. It was a classic case of dithering on my part, and then they were gone to leave me wishing that I had fired anyway; but I quickly forgave myself as I remembered that the concept of decoying was to get the birds in close – not to fire at long crossers.

145

As the light faded further another small pack came through, still not showing any interest in the decoys but this time a little closer. No dithering this time; instead a single accurate shot, with a dead teal floating in the water as the end result. This was to be the way of it during the short time before darkness closed right in, with few duck about, and those that did come were not terribly co-operative. A single teal bombed in over my left shoulder to plough up the water amongst the decoys. There it sat looking exceedingly nervous, so that it was airborne the instant I showed myself. But it was an easy shot, and fell back into the water before it had gone very far. One or two lone pintail kept tantalisingly out of harm's way – graceful stately birds so coveted by the bulk of wildfowlers. With four teal in the bag and most of the light gone I was entitled to feel quite contented, for I would most definitely have settled for a good deal less on a day which was designed more for escapism than serious wildfowling.

A single pintail came tacking across the wind, took a look at the decoys and as I sat up to fire began to turn away. By then I was committed and fired anyway at what was a fairly long-range bird; for a moment it seemed unscathed then staggered and spun down into the water a long way out. In the gloom the bird was only occasionally visible as a vague black bundle on the water, with the dog completely unsighted; even so this presented no problem as I let the wind blow it inshore and, after a few minutes, it was an easy task to take the dog along the shoreline from whence she gathered it with the minimum of fuss. It was a magnificent drake, resplendent in an unsullied plumage, and sporting very long black 'pin' feathers. Father Christmas had thus been very good to me, and the long wait for the tide to back off coupled with the weary

trudge back were not the chore they might have been if I had not put a few birds in the bag.

So to another yuletide; yet another enjoyable, if rather traditionally ineffective, Boxing Day shoot, and an impatient week waiting for the multitude to return to work and thereby leave the shore largely in peace. The morning flight on January First was bravely undertaken with a less than clear head, with a predictable lack of anything edible to show for the effort; nevertheless the New Year had been seen in, and with only seven short weeks remaining before the end of the season there was little time to waste.

—12—

By the Light of the Moon

I N CHAPTER 8 I REFERRED to a newly arrived skein of grey geese – European white-fronts in fact. If the reader was able to detect a tone of reverence in that passage, and elsewhere when I have had cause to mention grey quarry geese, then I make no apology for such a typically human failing; it is a genuine feeling of supreme admiration for this most magnificent of wildfowl quarry, and it is an emotion displayed by so many devotees of the sport.

I attempted to portray something of my sense of awe at that secret moment when they first arrive, but have to confess that this arrival can scarcely remain secret for very long. For even if they remain ever elusive, the grey geese can scarcely be ignored for very long: their presence is too outstanding, and they seem somehow determined to make their arrival as widely and as swiftly known as they possibly can. There can be no faster carrier of the news of their coming than the geese themselves, for thereafter they soar above the marshes and estuaries on mighty wings. Far-carrying vocal tones shout to all the world that the geese are back, and there will be many who are keen to hear this urgent message.

From that moment on, until the end of the season, it will be a ceaseless battle of wits between the quarry and that incredibly dedicated wildfowler – the wild goose hunter. To so many the goose is the supreme sporting challenge, and it is a challenge which will be eagerly taken up each season and pursued with a fanatical, single-minded determination which so thoroughly epitomises the wildfowler. To me, and to so many others, the goose will always be the ultimate quarry, and no amount of time and effort will be too great if a goose might be had at the final reckoning. Without question it may sometimes be a Herculean task to get on terms with these birds in a county where they are relatively scarce if one uses some of the Scottish or northern firths and estuaries as a datum. I have even heard it said that such a pursuit be as forlorn and wasteful a way of spending one's time as one could wish to come across, and this by wildfowlers of many years' standing. Such comments shock me, and even smack a little of the pot-hunter. Personally I do not know how any can resist the call of the wild grey geese – but then we are thankfully all different.

A wild goose chase

The wild goose hunt can be a frustrating experience in that post-holiday, early January period, for seldom do they seem to have settled into any sort of sensible pattern. Frequently the rare opportunities will occur as the reward for persistence, rather than by virtue of some shrewd or cunning manoeuvre; alternatively old habits and tried and trusted ambushes may once again come up trumps, even when logic says nay. Good wildfowling weather will sometimes be a great aid, but just as often it will prove of no assistance whatever. Curiously my best ever bag of white-fronts was attained in weather conditions which positively forbade such an achievement. How strange. It seems that only the wildfowler faithfully follows the recommended code of behaviour for all good sporting geese – most certainly the quarry seems loathe to do so on more than the odd occasion.

The pre-evening flight ritual of getting down to the coast early to 'glass' the fields for geese, in order to try and assimilate some sort of plan, will be an important part of January sport once the geese are well 'in'. Frequently this serves no other purpose than to set the adrenalin racing at the sight of the grazing flocks, with the actual flight out to roost remaining as problematical as it was before any goose-spotting had been carried out. But such reconnoitring is a traditional part of goose hunting hysteria, and I would not be denied it for the world.

Yet early January seldom yields the sort of massed flighting so typical of February and beyond. Admittedly the occasional mighty skein of yelping birds may come through, but for the most part one pursues smaller skeins or family parties. Curiously this does not make the prospects of a shot any less likely, with the opposite often being the case, for these small parties are easier to call and are apt to behave a little less cautiously than the massed battalions. So to lie in ambush in some favourite spot is as good an idea as any, even if the result will invariably be a succession of blanks. It is a question of values really – to me one goose in a dozen trips would be a worthwhile proposition, although for others perhaps such fortitude would be a little too much to ask; still others might deem a single goose ample reward for a whole season's work, and plenty of wildfowlers are denied even this slender crumb of comfort.

That January I went to the shore armed with trusty magnum and heavy loads on numerous occasions, but although I heard geese often enough they never once came near or by. Undaunted I persevered, for the period of the full moon approached and I knew that this would spell a temporary end to any prospect of a regular goose flight developing. One afternoon I went to the shore in sombre mood: the day was drab and overcast, with scarcely a breath of wind; the binoculars had revealed not a single goose on the usual feeding areas, which meant that the flocks were off feeding out of my immediate locale – something which was bound to substantially reduce the chances of a shot. I waited sullenly in a shallow creek and reflected on a fortnight of vigorous goose hunting without a single shot to show for my effort – truly a wild goose chase! The light had all but gone, with not a single star shining through the cloud cover above, whilst the spasmodic whistling of wigeon packs could be heard as they flighted in to feed. The occasional rush of wings where some speeding pack of waders passed close by caused momentary heart flutter, but there was not a bird of any sort to be seen.

The sudden appearance of six geese in close-knit order was therefore doubly surprising, whilst the fact that they were bearing down on me at a good shootable height caused me to crouch slowly into the creek bed, lest any hasty movement disturb them. They came on quickly enough – totally silent, almost as though they sensed that perhaps it was not entirely safe this close to the salting edge. But there could be no mistaking the slender-winged form of the white-fronted goose. A shattering experience this, the final moments as the skein draws within range: the pounding of the heart; the desperate fight to control quivering limbs, and the furious activity of the brain as one tries to judge the correct moment for action, so that the likelihood of this rare opportunity being wasted is reduced to a minimum. Now. Straighten up and fire in one smooth movement before they take alarm and begin to climb away. Everything has been judged to perfection, with the birds a mere 40 yards away and angled across the right shoulder, but no bird falls to the shot, and pandemonium ensues. The fearful crash of the heavy load is the first sign of danger to the cruising skein; then they are climbing almost vertically, their voices high-pitched and urgently proclaiming alarm and fear as the great threshing wings seek to distance the bulky frames from the menace which lurks below.

To the wildfowler the missed shot is a disaster – they seemed so easy, perhaps too easy. Then he too registers panic, lest the birds escape him completely and all his efforts come to nought. Then the muzzle is heaved upwards to overtake the climbing birds, and again the crash echoing back from the mud before the night swallows the geese up and only their wild voices remain as a reminder of their passing. But that second shot has sped true, and one of the skein lies crumpled on the mud. Gone is that deflatory emotion which so swiftly followed the first shot; in its stead is pure unbridled joy, with a fine bird brought to hand as a substantial reward for labour and persistence. That goose was not to be the last of that particular season but in many ways it was the most satisfying. This is so often the way of things, with success born out of a 'nothing' situation being savoured long after more premeditated events have receded into the darker recesses of the mind.

Thereafter with clearer skies and an ever-enlarging moon riding high in the sky at evening flight, the geese did not leave the fields at dusk, instead they preferred to use the extra light as a safeguard against night prowlers so that they could feed on with impunity. In the moonlight the grey geese can flight when it suits them to do so, rather than at the behest of a darkening sky. The noble birds are not slow to take advantage of such an opportunity, and during this period the uninitiated wildfowler can be driven near to distraction. Much earlier, in Chapter 8, I discussed some of the special problems related to wildfowling during the period of the full moon, although I confined my comments to the morning flight. Therefore it is fitting that I enhance the reader's knowledge of moonlight shooting without further delay.

Moonlight shooting

The full moon period will affect ducks as well as geese. In some instances this affect can be substantial, with the quality of sport altered out of all recognition. The normal flighting patterns may be severely disrupted, sometimes to the wildfowler's advantage, whilst equally often the opposite will apply. Where the moon is in the sky at dusk, ducks too will sometimes forsake the traditional evening flight; instead they will loaf out on the roost in nonchalant, unhurried manner – much to the disgust of the wildfowler waiting patiently for the flight. One of the great benefits at such a time is the ever-present likelihood that the birds will eventually flight in a long, drawn-out procession, sometimes lasting for hours, instead of the usually frantic rush at dusk. When this occurs, the wildfowler who is fortunate enough to be in the right place can enjoy some quite superlative sport.

Occasionally the flighting may begin at dusk and go on well into the evening, although such a spectacle is far less common than some storytellers would have us believe! Where a big moon and a late evening high tide combine, the chances of good sport will be much increased, for the flooding tide is apt to force birds from their roosts so that they will flight in dribs and drabs. When the moon is on the wane, and yet to rise at dusk, a split flight can occur, with some birds moving at dusk in the normal way whilst others sit out and await the rising of the moon. This is in some ways a curious phenomenon, with a post-evening flight lull heralding a renewed burst of energy almost as soon as the moon nudges its way over the horizon. Yet to attain any worthwhile moonlight flighting requires a high percentage of luck, with the various requisites needing to gel at the same instant if the gunner is to be rewarded. The big moon in isolation will not be enough to give the wildfowler adequate sporting opportunity, for without the correct cloud cover against which the birds will be silhouetted, the whole exercise will soon become futile and frustrating. There is nothing worse than being down on the shore under a giant moon, only for the birds to be invisible against a cloudless sky.

On those nights where a giant bright orb marches its remorseless way across the starry void, and where the only deviation from that inky monotony is the moon's own ghostly aura, it may be possible to be down on the shore all night long without catching so much as a glimpse of a bird! Yet, as with most rules, there will be exceptions where it will be possible to shoot – albeit on a limited basis. This occurs chiefly when the moon is low in the sky, so that a concentration of light may be found low above the horizon; under such conditions look for mud and water, where reflected light seems to enhance this effect and thereby multiplies the chance of getting some worthwhile shooting. Conversely too much cloud cover will of course blot out the moon completely, so that any attempt at flighting becomes completely thwarted. This will occur in any given season with depressing regularity, so that it is not at all uncommon for entire moons to be lost in this manner. What is required is a happy medium – something which will often be difficult to come across.

Ideally there needs to be a cottonwool-like layer of fluffy white clouds all across the sky, with enough of a breeze to keep the clouds moving across the moon in a delightful succession of light-giving layers. Under such conditions it will be possible to spot flighting birds at considerable distances. I well remember being advised, in far-off tyro days, that if you could see a duck in the moonlight then it would be within shooting range; long ago I learnt that this is not necessarily so, and in turn proffer my own advice that the Gun adjudge range in the normal manner.

The wildfowler's ears – always a vital part of his duck-detection equipment during the gloaming – will often give the first warning of approaching birds. Yet it is not uncommon for duck to suddenly arrive completely unannounced, so it will be necessary to remain constantly alert and ready for action; however, this may be easier said than done, especially when the wildfowler spends long spells on the shore or when the weather is extremely cold. Moonlight flighting can be a tense, and therefore draining, experience, and it is all too easy to get caught out; the likelihood of this occurring is increased when birds are few and far between, with concentration bound to waver. But I often think that the ability to concentrate depends on the person's recent experiences: any down-turns of fortune are apt to have a preoccupying, and therefore unsettling, effect; conversely, when things are going well and it feels good to be alive it is so much easier to feel at peace with the world and to concentrate on the job in hand – irrespective of what that job may be. I often feel that I should stay at home in a darkened room when 'bad vibes' assail me, although I never do of course and usually live to wish I had as one disaster follows upon another.

During that January moon few duck were using the saltings, or even flighting sensibly; the geese were safely ensconced on the fields, and things could scarcely have seemed gloomier for the wildfowler. Nonetheless, the compulsion to get down to the shore remained, even if there seemed little tangible reward available for such effort.

When your luck is in
One afternoon, with the moon just past the full, the sky was absolutely perfect with a subtle breeze causing the trees about the house to stir gently. Even if the likelihood of any decent shooting was remote, I had to be away, even leaving extra-early such was the wildfowling urge. It was not even particularly cold, and no great hardship to be out-of-doors on such a day. I could see no geese on the fields, and no more than a handful of teal on a wide fleet which often held good numbers of duck. Just a few coot and swans, whilst down on the shore the usual posse of shelducks were giving the *hydrobia* a hard time.

The high saltmarsh, with the cluster of tide pools at one end, which often encourages a small party of duck to rest there on quieter days, was empty, save for a restless flock of those squalid starlings. Momentarily, memories of youthful days engaged in slaughtering these verminous creatures on the autumn stubbles came to me, and caused me to smile, though scarcely with pleasure – rather from the memory of such carefree exuberance. Then the high saltmarsh was away behind me, and I was soon obliged to begin the seemingly interminable task of struggling across the broken salting and diffused areas of mud which lay around the larger creeks. The occasional redshank rose shrieking in alarm, one or two swinging round in a tormenting arc, mobbing the whole while – so that I was inclined to curse the sanctity afforded them by the notorious *1981 Act*!

The faint far off yodel of geese came down to me on the breeze so I now had a valid excuse for halting the self-torture of the salting hike. I soon spotted them as they appeared from behind the high ground to the east; they came on, very high, in a wavering line of almost 20 birds, on a heading which would bring them right overhead. At such times it is instinctive to dive for cover, even if the quarry is too high or too wide – for I have learnt time without number that anything can happen in this sport. The 'cover' took the form of a tiny cut in the edge of the salting into which I could push the dog, and lay prone across her, hoping we would be ignored even if we could scarcely hope to be invisible. Fortunately, the dog had endured this indignity many times before and reacted with no more than a derisory grunt. The frantic scramble to thrust heavy loads into the gun, just in case, assumed a new urgency as the geese began to noticeably lose height, almost as though the nearness of the mud had inspired them with a new-found confidence.

Suddenly there was a half-chance of a shot, where before none had existed, so I willed them to lose a little more height so they would be just within the limit of range. Even so it was hard to decide whether they were shootable or not, and I let them go over the brim of my floppy hat before I made any movement. When I sat up they were directly overhead, but very high indeed. No time to dally now. Just time to decide whether or not the shot was on. Two hard thumps as the magnums leapt from the muzzle, and an instant later the geese were climbing and breaking formation, whilst their voices registered the usual panic as in a moment they were borne to safety on those great wings. Incredibly a bird was falling, untidily at first, but then closing into a neater bundle as it plummetted down with a great swosh of air preceding the almighty smack as it half buried itself in the mud. It was quite dead, and so firmly embedded in the mud that I had to help the dog make the retrieve. It was a fine adult bird, with its breast a mass of black bars whilst the white forehead was crisp and clean. A very unlucky goose.

I seemed to float across the mud after that, and eventually sat in the saltings awaiting the coming of the night in a state of high euphoria. Now I did not care if anything came or not for I had enjoyed my share of luck for that day. But when your luck is in you can often do no wrong, and so it was to prove this day in most spectacular fashion.

In the last glimmer of daylight the only duck of the day came silently to the slushy salting edge. It was a slender teal that could have chosen the whole shore across which to flight, instead of this one small patch of light against which I spotted it with ease. I laid the tiny body alongside the goose amongst the *spartina* – truly the little and large of the wildfowl world. In that instant the moon nudged its yellow rim above the eastern horizon, and a short while later the fleecy clouds began to take on a lighter hue; it soon became a wondrous sky, although a complete lack of duck tended to make the whole exercise somewhat futile. But I was on a definite 'high', so sat on, not so much with any realistic hope of sport but more because it was so good to be on the shore, with the voices of the night birds all around.

I sat there indulgently recalling such nights from the past – some of which had been absolute sporting feasts, whilst others had been as duckless as this. The moon now rode ever higher, and the shore was alight from the glistening tideway to the ashen scar of the seawall.

Presently the stuttering voices of mallard announced the approach of a pair of birds from the direction of the inland marsh; they swept past me flying very low to the east, so I could see them a long way off. At my gentle, yet persistent, calling they swung beneath the moon in a lazy arc that brought them back towards me. It was a wonderful opportunity and I killed them both with a classic right and left – a duck and her handsome drake to lay with the goose and teal. Within a further 10 minutes I experienced something akin to those rather hackneyed T.V. action replays as another pair responded to my calling and also fell to a crisply delivered pair of shots. I could scarcely believe my good fortune, for this was like one of those improbable wildfowling daydreams come true. The evening was abruptly transformed from one of idle contemplation to an exciting flight as more mallard, albeit in singles and odd pairs, began to quarter the saltmarsh. What caused this sudden influx of birds I do not know, and have been quite unable to find a satisfactory explanation to this day; but, never one to look a gift horse in the mouth for very long, I added a further two birds from the chances on offer before deciding to pack in.

To shoot six mallard, a teal and a goose under conditions where it was optimistic to expect anything at all was, to say the least, little short of miraculous. I admit that I am not a great believer in miracles, but I most certainly had cause to thank that fortuitous goose for its contribution; for without such a massive boost to morale I should have left the shore with but a single teal in the bag, and probably thankful for that! I crammed all the duck into my sidebag, which was barely able to contain such a bulky cargo, whilst the goose would have to be carried swinging free in a spare hand – an awkward and inconvenient method of transportation, but one which I was obliged to suffer as I had not bothered to bring a larger bag. Thus readied I set off across the glistening expanse of the shore, with the gun tucked under the right arm.

Yet before I had gone more than a dozen paces a rapid fluttering of wings told of a startled duck, which a moment later reared from its line of flight and headed straight off down the line of salting edge. In a purely reflex action the goose was set free, the gun raised and fired in one smooth movement, and mallard number seven swooshed onto the shore. That was enough! While the dog made yet another retrieve, I unloaded and slid the gun into its case, so that no further temptation might conspire to add to my heavy load. What an incredible evening. Truly my cup runneth over!

—13—

When the Cold Winds Blow

I T SELDOM CEASES TO amaze me how the highly-paid weather wizards, backed by millions of pounds' worth of sophisticated equipment, can get their forecasts wrong with such astonishing regularity! Admittedly for the most part they will be reasonably accurate; but when the chips are really down, with some violent weather change in the offing, they invariably foul up. (No pun intended there!) To the wildfowler the prevailing weather conditions are of the utmost importance, for so often his sport will be influenced by conditions on his local shore. It is a point which I have already made elsewhere in this book, although I do not feel that I over-stressed its importance – indeed the reverse might well be the case.

Although it may seem difficult for the tyro to comprehend, weather conditions elsewhere – indeed even in other countries – will have its effect on our sport. Indeed migration itself is a direct result of birds responding to adverse weather conditions, for the mass exodus to the warmer south does not occur each year because the birds need the exercise. Yet once migration has settled down and the flocks have established themselves in suitable winter quarters, there they will invariably stay until something prompts them to move. Usually one of three factors precipitates a move: a scarcity of food; disturbance at an unacceptable level, or severe, adverse weather conditions. Where the latter occurs those wildfowlers living in more southerly parts of the country might find themselves inundated with hordes of weather migrants, which may arrive from further north or even from mainland Europe. This can be a boon time for wildfowlers, although this may in turn create special problems of which I shall write in a moment.

Because of the perversities of British weather it will not always be the most northerly regions which will receive the worst of the weather. In the winter of 1986/87 appalling conditions paralysed the south and east of England, whilst the north and Scotland remained relatively mild. This is not the first time that such a phenomenon has occurred in recent years and rather overturns traditional thinking with regard to our weather patterns.

Effects of hard weather

Hard weather (by which I mean prolonged spells of frost and/or snow) is often the answer to a wildfowler's prayers. It is apt to be a happy time for the wildfowler prepared to endure the inevitable hardships to be encountered on the freezing shore, and is likely to provide better than average opportunities for putting a few birds in the bag. Quite simply where such conditions prevail the inland slushes and waterways soon become frozen over, whilst much greenery may be covered in snow. At such times the shore, guaranteed the twice daily thawing action of the tide, will remain relatively clear so that legions of wildfowl may quickly congregate in some areas. The wildfowler will take advantage of such an occurrence, and quite rightly so, but any wildfowler worthy of the name will not do so to excess. Most wildfowlers are fine and honourable sportsmen and would not dream of perpetrating the sort of slaughter which is undoubtedly possible on some occasions. This is a tense and vulnerable time for wintering flocks, and during prolonged spells of such weather birds may lose condition and even ultimately depart for other, milder parts.

The need for restraint at such times is widely recognised and practiced within the wildfowling fraternity, with few reported incidents of any abuses occurring. A general feeling of responsibility to the quarry is one reason for such an attitude, whilst the desire to avoid any wanton wastage of what is, after all, the wildfowl stock for future years also figures high in the final reckoning. Increasingly, in modern times the influence of wildfowling clubs, with the BASC heading the list, has played a considerable part in ensuring that the quarry gets the best possible deal – with the worst hit areas often the subject of voluntary wildfowling suspensions. Much good may be derived from such enforced measures in terms of conservation credibility and good public relations, but most especially of all it gives wild birds a respite when they need it the most.

Amongst the less reprehensible provisions of the *Wildlife and Countryside Act 1981* is the statutory right for the Secretary of State for the Environment to sign an order suspending wildfowling under certain hard weather criteria. Obviously any such legislation will be fraught with problems, with anomalies and unfairnesses inevitable, and I do not propose to deal with the subject in anything other than a superficial manner – and this only to give some balance to this particular narration of our sport. Basically such criteria is tied into the 'state of ground' reports as determined by a set number of meteorological stations sited around the coasts. After several days of frozen or snow-covered ground the countdown will begin which will lead to the Nature Conservancy Council recommending a statutory suspension of wildfowling for a given period. Of course precise numbers of days for each part of the procedure exist as I write, but as these have only recently been revised and will undoubtedly be continually altered in the future, to quote these will be a purely academic exercise which will be of little benefit to anyone.

One of the best facets of this new criteria is its flexibility and the fact that the wildfowling community is allowed a substantial input into what amounts to an ongoing review of the criteria. The BASC, ably backed by its network of local wildfowling clubs, is part of a team which includes the NCC and the RSPB and which periodically sets about analysing the way the system works. Of the various unfairnesses inherent in the system, the blanket suspension of sport finds the least favour with wildfowlers. There is much merit in the argument favouring some sort of regionalisation of suspensions, but one must temper such thoughts with realism. How and where would such demarcation lines be drawn? Who would have the onerous task of deciding such regional boundaries? Undoubtedly further unfairnesses would arise, and perhaps might even provoke more arguments than the present system. Personally I would hate to see the sort of lunacy prevail which at present applies to the variable Sunday shooting regulations: here some counties debar Sunday shooting, whilst neighbouring counties give the go-ahead; thus you can shoot wildfowl in one county on a Sunday, but not in the next a few inches away!!

So, on balance, I believe the present system should remain, subject to the continuance of a substantial wildfowling input. However, I do agree wholeheartedly with the many responsible wildfowling clubs, and BASC individual members, who contend that they do not need oppressive Government legislation to ensure they behave in the correct manner; but, as in all things, the force of law is undoubtedly necessary to guarantee the compliance of a tiny rogue minority who feel answerable to no man.

Standards vary enormously amongst folk, and the definition of what constitutes a bird in poor condition is no exception. To many the actual physical condition of birds is considered the supreme arbiter, so that only if the birds are losing weight rapidly should we consider them no longer worthy of sport. To me this is a load of eye-wash. I believe that it is increased vulnerability – regardless of physical condition – which should determine when wildfowl shooting should be restricted. A fine yardstick is when any rag-a-muffin wildfowler, regardless of expertise, starts to bring home above average bags – surely then the birds are approaching a suicidal state and a halt should be called

A cold morning flight

That hard, cold January, as the moon waned with ever-increasing rapidity, the frosts began to clamp down. It was mostly bright, clear, yet cold, during the day, but bitterly cold at night; a cruel icy hand soon gripped the inland marshes, so that even the largest fleets remained constantly frozen. Surprisingly this forced few extra birds onto the shore in search of food, and I hoped for a layer of snow to cover most of the remaining wildfowl foods. My memory, and faithfully accurate diary, told me of a similar winter when a large fleet provided the only open water for miles, and I had enjoyed some good, if short-lived, sport. So not unnaturally I set up a morning flight at the same place, hoping for a repeat performance.

Overnight the frost had again been severe, but now a gloomy darkened sky and a freshening easterly wind carried a dire warning of snow to come. Once on the saltings that wind whipped in off the sea like a knife, numbing any exposed flesh with some sort of demonic relish against which there was little defence. Under such circumstances only the indomitable spirit of the wildfowler prevents him from fleeing the shore, to take refuge of sorts in more sheltered parts. But even the darkness could not hide the frozen surface of the fleet, and it was a long disheartening wait until daylight for the birds which I knew were not coming. Come full light I lifted my frozen frame from the tiny creek, which had provided me with scant cover throughout my vigil, and shuffled over to the seawall for a reconnoitre of sorts. The wind was picking up the whole while, so the sea, even in its low tide state, was being chased into a frenzy of white-capped water, whilst inland the whole marsh was white with frost.

I stood splay-legged, in order to withstand the buffeting of the wind, on the seawall and glassed for open water – but there was none. It was a totally dispiriting sort of morning, with not a bird moving on the whole wide vista of the shore, save for the occasional ragged flight of cormorants moving in to feed, and the likelihood of any sport could not have appeared more remote. Yet, even as I stood there, a single wigeon came batting through at a good height, flying incredibly fast before the wind, to sweep down on a long searching scan of the marshes. But it had no more luck in its apparent search for open water than I, and soon turned back once more for the sea; now it flew a matter of feet above ground level, in an effort to evade the worst of the wind, only rising in order to clear the seawall. Thereafter it flew low across the mud before turning to the east and following the tideline off into the distance. From my modest vantage point I had witnessed the whole episode in graphic detail. It had been a marvellously coloured cock bird, resplendant in flashing white wing patches that are so indicative of the male of this species; where he was headed now I did not know, but was grateful that he had in a sparse manner enlivened my morning.

Now a flight began to develop, with two more singletons following the line of that first bird with remarkable precision. The wind blew harder, and seemingly colder, so that it was hardly surprising that any birds out on the open shore should want to find somewhere a little more hospitable. Even though I had no way of knowing whether or not the flight would come to anything, or fizzle out as suddenly as it had started, I had to try to take advantage of the situation – after all the sport of wildfowling is built around speculation. The struggle out across the mud to where a few isolated clumps of *spartina* grew was a bitter contest against a gale that now tugged at the clothing, and burst inside my balaclava as it determined to freeze me and thereby undermine my resolve. If this was the wind's intention then it failed miserably, for little can deter a wildfowler if he thinks he may be able to get under a few wigeon.

By any normal standards the cover was scarcely adequate to hide both man and dog in broad daylight, but the morning was hardly normal and I might just stand a chance against the low-flying wigeon. Another bird went off downwind, to disappear beyond the seawall. Dutifully I waited, and sure enough, before too long, it flipped over the seawall and came on a zero altitude. It was a case of remaining tucked down into the cold and spiky *spartina* until the last possible moment before sitting up for the shot. The shot was a long one, but the bird saw me late and had barely begun to react when the shot sent it spinning down onto the mud. Almost immediately a pack of half-a-dozen swept off inland, only to return in short order, as if totally unimpressed by the inhospitable scenery

161

below them. This time they came straight to me, so the first shot was an easy one; then the pack was exploding upwards with the wind aiding their escape, but I was fortunate enough to tickle another out with my third shot.

Another cock came right over me, but this time my timing was awry and even the second shot only clipped him, so that he went down across the mud to crash some 60 or 70 yards out amongst the boiling waves. I sent the dog, even though she was hopelessly unsighted, and, although she battled desperately for her retrieve, she eventually returned with nothing. Yet this was no great problem, as the bird was dead and with an onshore wind I sent her into the shallows further along the shore some 10 minutes later to finish the job. After a further half an hour in the squalid mess of a hide amongst the *spartina*, and with two more fine wigeon in the bag, I gave it best. I had conjured six wigeon from a nothing situation, and was well content not to overdo it. All had been fine sporting birds, taken in the finest traditions of the sport – real hard weather wildfowling.

Snow storm

That afternoon the snows came. Heavy enough to cover almost everything inland, yet not bad enough to prevent my rather tentative drive to the shore on the following day for what I planned as an all-day session. The weather was showing no sign of breaking, and a wildfowling suspension was only a couple of days away; even though the birds still seemed in good condition I did not baulk at such a thought, yet remained determined to get a few more providing they were not giving themselves up. My rucksack was well stocked: soup, coffee, spare gloves, plenty of cartridges, and a pair of mallard decoys – just in case I should have need of them. The load was heavy, and the walk a long and arduous affair even though the snow lay only a couple of inches deep; but that wind was so unbelievably cold that it almost took the breath away – here was truly a wind born somewhere up on the Arctic Circle, and losing none of its venom on the long journey south.

At my destination hundreds of wigeon greeted me in the eerie first gloom of dawn; indeed three excellent chances came my way in rapid succession, all of which I declined for the very best of reasons. Quite simply the chances had been at birds making off across a partially flooded creek, and I had no intention of asking the dog to get wet through so early in the day's proceedings. A wildfowler's dog is expected to endure much on his behalf, so an occasional act of consideration is the least we can do in return.

Anyway there seemed plenty of birds about, and I soon had a couple of mallard down on relatively dry ground – safely and easily retrieved before being stowed away. As is invariably the case, the dawn revealed several thousand wigeon feeding further down the coast where I could not get at them; but there was still plenty moving in my area, and even if the sport was never fast and furious it was most certainly of the very highest calibre.

Beyond any doubt the colour of the sky was the most striking feature of that morning flight: never have I seen such a dark brooding sky, positively bulging with snow as if eager to throw its evil storm upon the shore. The wind rose to fever pitch, hurtling out of the east so that it slapped into my left ear as if quite contemptuous of the scant protection offered by my woollen balaclava. Eventually this was to cause me a great deal of discomfort, and added another dimension to the sort of suffering directly attributable to wildfowling under such austere conditions. The wigeon were all packed in together on a long finger of salting, with only the occasional pack coming my way; even so these stayed well out of range with only mallard providing any chance of sport. As the tide ran out to virtually nothing so the snow began to fall: first a few pathfinding flakes, falling diagonally across the shore as swiftly as minute hurtling meteors. Then the great storm clouds were overhead and the snow came like a dense white blanket, to reduce visibility to a few yards in next to no time.

Without exception I have never been out in such a storm before. The snowflakes seemed as large as a fingernail, and of a density almost impossible to describe, so soon everything was covered. I brushed the dog clear countless times, whilst the snow piled up on me and all my gear – I must have been virtually invisible to any passing bird. This was worse than trying to shoot in dense fog, but I managed to get two more mallard as they flew blindly into the teeth of the storm. But most of the time I could do no better than cower in my tiny hovel in the salting edge praying for the snow to stop. Okay, I had hoped for a layer of snow to perhaps improve sport – but this was ridiculous.

After perhaps a couple of hours the storm began to abate, then the snow had moved on to whiten other lands off to the west. In its stead it left a shore which was a total white-out; even the saltladen muds were powerless when confronted by such blind ferocity, and lay inert and submissive under a virginal white layer. Only a single brown finger of water, trickling gently as a last reminder of the vanished tide – which alone amongst Nature's elements could have remained impervious to the storm – broke the white monotony.

Into this narrow channel I deposited my pair of decoys, for I now knew that this would be a certain draw for any approaching bird. So it was to prove, and I had just cause to be thankful for both decoys and artful use of a range of calls; admittedly many times birds saw me as the full daylight of a bright winter's day exposed the inadequacy of my position, but for a few the realisation that Man lurked close by came too late.

With many shots being at maximum range as birds turned quickly away, I was thankful of the special 1½ oz loads of No.6 shot, loaded for me by a friend. The killing power of these loads seems quite incredible. A single mallard drake stands out in the memory as a very spectacular shot indeed: he came warily after a couple of thoughtful circuits, and was turning away even as I sat upright for the shot, but a fierce swing and a huge lead poleaxed him at maximum range. What a shot! Four teal, following the grubby water from a long way back, rather like low-level fighter planes, lost a pair of birds to a neat right and left. Then four wigeon did the same, for me to get another pair. On the other side of the coin a single kamikaze shoveler evaded three shots with ease – and for all I know still lives to this day.

In so many ways it was a memorable, indeed extraordinary, day. Of course, most memorable was the weather; not just the wind either, but the deep biting cold generated by that wind. I do not know what the 'wind chill factor' – to use a modern parlance – was but it was in many ways a nightmare of a day to live through. I have often considered myself to be a tough little fellow, mostly capable of tolerating anything that the weather can serve up, with the exception of excessive heat, but on this day I would have defied anyone to remain oblivious to the conditions. After the snow had abated, conditions became in many ways even worse. The snow froze in icy globules in the dog's coat; also in my balaclava, and matted and froze my beard. I consumed food, drink and soup, grudgingly shared with a balefully staring gundog, and still could not shift the cold that seemed to permeate my very bones. The cold came in spasms which brought me to an uncontrollably shivering ruin, but I knew this would pass to be superseded by a burning sensation, before slipping into something akin to a numbing neutral condition.

After the snow, huge numbers of wigeon, mallard and shoveler flew around as though in a daze and waders stood around on the snowy mud looking thoroughly miserable. A single sleek hawk, a merlin I thought, nipped over the seawall behind me, and almost immediately what must have been a second merlin took a freezing dunlin from the mud and made off to the accompaniment of a fearful protest from the other waders nearby. At least one bird had no intention of starving.

In the afternoon the tide began to push up the creek once again, pushing the snow into a brown murky mess along its scummy edge. Twice I had to send the dog across the widening waters for birds, but soon decided to give it best for the storm clouds were gathering once again and the first giant flakes were beginning to fall. It would be a long struggle back and I wanted to make at least part of the trip in the fading light. Soon the snow came driving with stinging force into my face, for this way lay home and I had to take the full fury of the storm head on. The rucksack was unbearably heavy, for I had shot well despite the cold, with the bulk of the bag being made up of mallard – and most of these gaudy drakes. Constantly my load threatened to pull me over backwards, with each creek looming as a massive obstacle. More than once I fell, but struggled on as indeed I had to if I were to survive. It may seem strange to mention survival in safe old England, but such a storm can kill as surely as if it were in the Arctic. Let no man who has not endured such a phenomenon sneer, for my very survival was open to question before an eventual safe return.

The wigeon were packed on the flooding tide like a massive black oil slick, their voices coming as a cacophony of whistles even overpowering the rush of the wind such was the congregation of birds. Then, with the bulk of my journey still before me, the evening flight began. Wigeon, flighting hard against the wind, heading for some frugal fare on a huge field of rape blown partially clear by the wind, were slung all across the snow-filled sky; sometimes the packs were small, but mostly they came in great waves numbering hundreds of birds. I half fell into a muddy, snow-shrouded creek, mostly to rest but also to watch the flight. I tried one half-hearted shot, which missed quite comfortably; then realised with horror what I was doing, for the last thing that I needed was to increase my load any further – so the gun was thrust into its slip for the last time that day. The flight went on and on, so that eventually I resumed my journey with birds still pouring overhead, flighting desperately to the rape before the snow covered it completely. Normally this walk would take an hour and a quarter at maximum, but this day it became a three hour nightmare in a world of raging wind and dashing, blinding snow. Foolishly, as I became hotter and hotter still, I undid or removed various parts of my weatherproof clothing, so that the snow found its way in with even greater ease to add wetness to my other discomforts. A huge snowdrift, quite invisible to me in the lee of a seawall, almost engulfed me as I plunged straight into it up over my waist, before wallowing manfully on to where the snow lay only a foot or so deep. Increasingly came the desire to stop and rest, which I did at every opportunity, taking advantage of any minute windbreak. The desire to just sit there and sleep became almost overwhelming, but I was well aware of the consequences of such an action, and each time fought back the desire before once again soldiering on.

The van stood shrouded in snow, seemingly forlorn in the eerie lighting of the nearby inn, but a welcoming sight nonetheless. But the snow had blown in under the bonnet and it steadfastly declined to start until the battery was all but done in. Eventually, with a good deal of help, I was to get underway, but not before a lengthy spell of recuperation in the warm interior of that life-saving inn. The publican was horror-stricken, and tells people to this day that he thought I was going to die. Strictly between you and me, so did I at one time there. To spend a wretched 13 hours out on a frozen, wind-racked shore must rank alongside many more flamboyant adventures in terms of endurance. Perhaps I behaved foolishly, but I think not and would do the same again – indeed have done so since! But quite possibly a less experienced wildfowler would have succumbed; it is not possible to say, only to urge others to be equally well prepared before attempting such an adventure. To risk death for a bag of duck may seem to be taking the sport to extremes, and I would agree – but any likelihood of ending my wildfowling 'career'

had scarcely entered my head before setting out on that snowy morning.

For the complete wildfowler such is all part of his sport. We scarcely ask for danger, nor fly boldly in its face, but will gladly court all manner of perils if a bag is likely as reward.

—14—

The Tide

THROUGHOUT THESE MANY pages I have written with awe and often reverence of the shore, its composition and its inhabitants; of the elements, which are so oblivious to Man's presence, and indeed of everything that has its effect, no matter how slight, upon our sport. I do so advisedly and many of similar ilk will hopefully agree with me.

The sort of weather conditions described in Chapter 13 are far from the norm; indeed, the weather can be as kind as it is cruel, and can therefore scarcely claim credit as the supreme arbiter of life on the shore. This accolade must surely belong to the tide itself, for none other amongst Nature's weaponry possesses such consistently relentless power. The tide is life itself to so many of the organisms which live on or near the shore – be they minute or gigantic. But this purveyor of life can bring death as swiftly and as readily – the tide will flood where it will and woe betide anything which attempts to stand in the way. Of the natural phenomenon which I have thus far experienced, the tide is by far the most outstanding, in fact it could easily defy description such is its magnificence. But if the writer has any uses at all it is via the descriptive power of the pen, so that an attempt must always be made, irrespective of the subject.

The typical estuary scene at low tide will reveal an apparently sparse scattering of waders all across the wide acres of mud; only when the tide first rumbles its warning from the deep, and begins that remorseless forward march which will only cease at the high water mark, do the birds begin to display any sense of urgency or purpose. This is the time when the spectator will first gain some real impression of numbers, as the birds hurry to the tide edge to reap the bountiful harvest created by the advancing waters. Frequently they will busy themselves in great clouds of many thousands – all retaining a tenuous hold upon the shore until even their long legs can no longer act as a foil against the tide. Slowly the feeding flocks will be driven from one stretch of mud to the next, so the air will be filled with their thronging multitudes. Yet such movements are never haphazard or as unco-ordinated as they may seem, for there is a determination and sense of purpose in their flight as they seek to feed for the maximum possible time and only then retire to the roosts.

Finally the mud will all be awash, with the water into or over the saltings, dependant on height of tide. Then the waders will roost on the higher saltmarsh or off on the open coastal fields, where they wait in tight-packed stoic ranks for the ebb and a renewed feast upon the newly washed muds. It is then, with the ebb, that the most spectacular wader movements will be seen. The timing of the first small parties, often dunlin or redshank, is impeccable, for they diligently skim the salting edge impatiently waiting for the first landing pad to open up for them; then, at the first hint of a feeding site, they will be down, running and probing eagerly before the food has vanished back into some subterranean lair. Once the tide has drawn back from the salting edge the main wader battalions appear soon enough, drawn by the life force of the shore.

Those that have roosted far off inland appear as vague puffs of smoke, only taking on some plausible shape as they draw swiftly closer. Soon they will be overhead, the air filled with the rush of racing pinions and the seemingly excited voices of the speeding flock, before they dive to the exposed muds to feast greedily along the receding edge. Still others twist and turn in tightly-packed flocks low above the rippling waters in perfect unison, alternately showing brown backs or flashing pale underside as they turn. It is something of a puzzle how they can perform such faultless manoeuvres with such precision, but puzzle or not this does not make the event any less exciting. Suddenly, as if at some signal, they will all be down on the mud, running and dibbling furiously. There seems to be an infectious enthusiasm about them, rather akin to the delight exuded by excited children rushing to some long awaited party. The waders come in all sizes, with legs and bills as varied and diverse as one could possibly imagine. They come in what seems a never-ending stream – a concourse of whirring wings and of shrill piping voices. The shore waders are a totally fascinating and absorbing group of birds, and long may our estuaries continue to sustain such huge numbers.

The movement of the tide will also affect the ducks and the brent geese. See the ducks as they come to guzzle amongst the flooding saltings, reaping a rich harvest whilst the pickings are at their easiest. They will splash and preen; standing on their tails, in the manner so common amongst waterfowl, to the accompaniment of furious wing-flapping. At the ebb, if they remain relatively undisturbed, they may stay in the edge of the saltmarsh; but much more commonly they will idly drift away on the tide, to loaf out on the open sea until it is once again time for the flighting. The saw-bills, such as mergansers and goosanders, can be seen commonly enough flighting swiftly from one feeding place to another – their rapidly beating wings carrying that traditional sawbill shape of head-neck-body-tail all in line on some frenetic journey. Again no thought of a quarry, but these birds are an integral part of the estuary scene.

So too is the splendidly bizarre shelduck; indeed this bird is tied as closely to the estuary as are the waders, with the tide totally dictating its lifestyle. Soon after the retreat of the tide the shelduck can be found in small parties, or larger spread-out groups, eagerly sifting through the sloppiest muds with that perfectly adapted, Donald Duck-like bill! Watch as it struts almost pompously, like some austere old gentleman with his hands clasped firmly behind his back, across the mud with long neck lowered so that the bill can be worked industriously from side to side in search of food. The familiar, fern-like pattern so regularly found on the mud is irrefutable proof that a shelduck has been this way. The brent goose, of which I have written elsewhere, is a noisy, exuberant part of the story of the tide, and few could ignore its presence for very long. The story of the tide is one of perpetual motion, as it constantly disturbs or makes way for a whole succession of birds. Yes indeed, the tide is life itself.

If writers have waxed lyrical about the elements down the ages, so too have the composers – often with spectacular effect. Most of us will be familiar with the dramatic comparisons of the most impressive of elements, such as the wind and storm and ugly raging seas; but the sea is not always in ugly mood, for at times it will be intensely peaceful – as though it were a great giant asleep. Doubtlessly music exists to match the tide in lazy mood; to match the relentless making of the tide as it floods the flats to hurry the birds before it, and to compare with the diverse protestations of the feathered multitudes as they head for drier parts. It is, for me, the *Bolero*.

I have often wondered if it was the movement of the tide which so inspired the madness in Maurice Ravel to produce his brilliant piece, and this could so easily have been so. For just as the tide turns in the deep softly, almost imperceptibly, so the *Bolero* begins lightly, almost inaudibly. Then the tide begins its march, slowly covering more and yet more of the shore – the mud flats, sand bars and gaunt mussel beds – and in turn disturbing increasing numbers of birds. Its presence becomes ever more noticeable, whilst the rippling waters flood and sparkle all along the shallows, to inundate all before them. So too the *Bolero* makes its presence felt: rippling like those waves in a series of repetitions, yet increasingly swelling in volume as more and more instruments are brought into the piece. So easy to liken each instrument to the urgent voice of some disturbed wading bird: perhaps the warble of the curlew is the clarinet; the redshank can only be a flute, whilst the spectacular fanfare of the massed flocks of oystercatchers can only be the trumpet. The list is long, and a fitting inspiration for he blessed with a vivid imagination. Finally when the tide is into the shallows the brent geese come surging with resounding tones, that suggest a pulsation created by the trombone.

So the tide, after stalking the muds for hours with infinite patience, nears the seawall – the *Bolero* its climax. As the waves go rippling all across the last of open muds it is not difficult to imagine – almost see – Ida Rubinstein dancing to the crashing refrain of the *Bolero*. Her feet are immersed in the white foam at the water's edge: she is dancing to the music of the waves; dancing to the music of the birds as they finally flee to the high tide roosts, dancing ceaselessly to the *Bolero*. The end is very near. As the tide crashes upon the stones at the foot of the seawall, or flays the salting edge, so the *Bolero* crashes out louder and more magnificent with each stroke of the conductor's baton. Then, with complete suddenness, the *Bolero* is ended.

Here the comparison is ended too, for the story of the tide has no end. Soon it will slink back across the muds until it once again nestles somberly in the deep; like some giant magnet it will draw the wild birds in its wake – there is no rest for the tide, and seemingly little rest for the birds which must follow its dictates. Once in the deep the tide will merely pause, before remorselessly starting forward once again. Then, as the tide begins to flood, one can almost hear the conductor tap his baton and, as the first gulls are disturbed, the *Bolero* will begin again. Whilst the waders idle away that high tide period in a rare prolonged spell of relative inactivity there is still plenty to see as I have outlined variously but particularly in Chapter 10. Even the most innocuous of events reveals a deeper meaning, if we care to search diligently enough for it; indeed it is a worthwhile pursuit, for from this can only come a wider knowledge and therefore a greater sense of enjoyment – which is after all why we go to the coast in the first place.

Early season sights

The early season is a good time for such blissful study, before the days become shorter and colder and we tend more towards a vigorous pursuit of our sport. Long days can often be treated as lazy days during which we might find a greater fulfillment. Often one might see a brief glimpse of sleek fin knifing through the surface of the shallow water amongst the saltmarsh. Alternatively there may come a sizeable splash where a fish has briefly risen, to leave behind a rapidly spreading circle of ripples which gradually disappear until the surface of the water returns to its mirror-like calmness. One seldom sees very much more. Yet if the wildfowler remains very still he may be surprised at the sight of a fair-sized fish. This creature has been the bane of many an angler, and has acquired something of a reputation for being virtually uncatchable; of course this is a nonsense, as many a highly successful specialist can testify, but few fish possess an appetite as fickle as that of the grey mullet. Many an ambitious angler has gone home empty-handed and disappointed after trying a wide variety of baits to no avail.

There are some birds that take their food from the very waters of the estuary, and I cite two examples which may well be viewed as beauty and the beast. To take beauty first is a typically human failing, and this is a charge to which I must plead guilty, so I take the summer-visiting little tern as a first example. To the eye this bird may often seem like some overgrown white swallow as it hawks the shallows on slender flickering wings. Despite its size the species is so typical of all the terns, for it exudes grace and beauty in its every movement. It will hunt its prey – some tiny shrimp or other – from a vantage point low above the waves, alternately hovering, moving on and hovering again before plunging bodily into the waters, waters from which it flies without any apparent hesitation or hinderance.

The voice is the usual tern screech, though lacking something of the raucous noise generated by the larger common tern. Yes, the terns seem to love their fishing; perhaps this love is only surpassed by the delight which they show in the aerial piracy which is so common, or by their furious mobbing and scolding of any intruder that dares to come too close. In many parts the screech of the terns, and the harsher tones of black-headed gulls, are as much a part of the late summer shore as is the warble of the first curlew or the plaintive air of the grey plover. But soon, long before the coming of the first frosts, the little tern will have fled to far off, warmer climes and, in common with such as the garganey and the summering 'shanks, will not see these shores again for another few months.

Each and every splash in the tideway tells its own story – for a splash will have been created by some creature or other, and will therefore warrant some investigation. Seldom will one be disappointed, unless the search is for the highly unusual and nothing less.

For the beast read cormorant, as I can think of few uglier versions of Nature's work on the shore. I have little love for the cormorant, for he gives the impression of being an evil, verminous bird – indeed, in many ways such an impression is well justified. He is a vast, near-black decimator of the fish stocks, and in extreme cases where numbers are excessive, can seriously damage a fishery. The protection of the cormorant under the *1981 Act* seems to make little sense, for often a limited cull was regarded as a necessity for hard-pressed inshore fishermen. Watch the cormorant in flight, invariably in the company of others of its own kind, and it is massive, almost goose-like – save for the longer tail, and heavy laboured flight. There is nothing remotely elegant about the cormorant in flight, whilst the actual take-off is reminiscent of some dilapidated, severely over-laden bomber; it is something of wonder that the cormorant is capable of flight at all.

But to see the cormorant in the water is a different story, for here it exudes the sort of stylish confidence so obviously absent when in the air. See him swimming in that typical low-in-the-water manner; the neck is long and snakelike, topped with that ugly head and cruel bill – a superbly adapted fishing machine. Then he is gone, diving in search of food. Often the search is fruitless, but often enough the bird will surface with some victim writhing in the vice-like grip of that fearsome bill. Perhaps the victim will be a small flatfish, a flounder, or perhaps a dab, but often it will be a silver eel. How fascinating is this, the death of a silver eel – one moment it is frantically wriggling and flashing in the sunlight in a last desperate attempt to retain its tenuous grip on life, the next it is gone. In a few spasmodic jerks of that gruesome head and neck the eel has been condemned to follow the journey of so many of its kind – into a foul acid-filled stomach. Perhaps it is churlish to mourn the death of a single eel – but my loathing for the cormorant doubtlessly serves to cloud my emotions. Yet the cormorant has his rights to the fruits of the estuary, and has his own, no doubt vital, place in the great scheme of things.

Now watch the cormorant standing inelegantly on some low island, or stark man-made, yet frequently derelict, structure, with wings spread wide in order to dry the sodden feathers. Time marches on in the estuary and on the shore, irrespective of beauty or ugliness. The cormorant can help himself to the contents of the murky waters, and to as much time as he may need to dry those feathers before the next fishing trip. Only Man puts such a premium on time, for there will never be enough to complete this fascination of the shore.

—15—

Farewell The Shore

A FTER MY LITTLE adventure in the snow, which could so easily have cost me very dearly indeed, the expected wildfowling suspension came into effect. Not that this bothered me unduly as I was something of a spent force for a few days anyway; in terms of birds in the bag I had also had enough to keep me happy, and was quite content to spend a couple of weeks in contemplation of recent events.

When the suspension was eventually lifted most of the snow and ice had thawed, leaving the landscape crisp and clean – if a little ragged in places where vegetation had been pounded flat. But the nights were still very cold, with enough of a frost to produce some superficial freezing. Only one day of the inland season remained, so I had the choice of a final foray inside the seawall, or a flight on the shore itself. In neither case were the prospects particularly encouraging, but as there would be a further 20 days of wildfowling opportunity on the shore I elected to try the inland option.

Inland shooting

In the mid-afternoon I went off to a small shoot where I had a Gun at the time. It consisted of several large pools – occasioned by flooded gravel workings – and a small area of freshmarsh which often held a small area of floodwater at the backend of the season; after all the melting snow there was a flood extending to about half-an-acre, so that was the evening flight organised. Additionally there was often the chance of picking off the odd diving duck, tufted or pochard, around the pools, although a good wind was usually required to maximise any opportunity. This day there was no more than a stiff breeze blowing, with a clear sky as the

Another bird safely retrieved.

harbinger of the frost to come, so that the chances of finding any duck sheltering under the steep banks was not good. Nonetheless, duty dictated a series of fruitless stalks, whilst a few dozen tufted loafed insolently in the centre of the largest pool.

Finally luck rewarded my persistance as two superb drake tufted burst from the lee of a small clay island to cross me at maximum range. The realisation that this would probably be my one and only chance added power to my swing, so that the lead bird plummetted into the water with a big splash; the second shot was a purely instinctive reaction, and amazingly this bird fell also. Quite possibly one of my very best right-and-lefts at duck. Yet fate has a way of delivering a rapid smack to any smug face which chances to show itself, and so it was this day. As expected the shots scattered the remaining duck, and in the resultant confusion a single tufted flew directly overhead, and very low indeed, but was totally unscathed by my three shots.

The dog swam for the first bird, even though it was a long way out, but the second bird had drifted too far and I saw no point in asking for such a long-distant retrieve when it was a simple task to walk around the pool and wait for the bird to drift in. This was done, and in the process I even managed to add another tufted to my bag; so three plump birds, when expectations had been for an absolute zero, put morale at a high ready for the evening flight.

So with the light already beginning to fade I took the slain back to the car, collected a bag full of decoys and made my way to the flood. Soon the decoys were set out in the shallow water and, even though there was no cover at all, I made myself comfortable on a minute knoll of higher ground. If any birds came whilst it was still half-light they would be certain to see me, so my best chance would be if birds came with the light all but gone. There were a few dapper little upturned mallard preenings in the margins of the flood, as clear a sign of recent visitors as one could possibly find, so there was every likelihood of a shot or two, but in all honesty I did not care a jot – for the season was dying now, and it was just good to be out on the wide empty marsh.

For me this is one of the most poignant moments of the entire season: a time for nostalgic reminiscence of the weeks and months of stimulating pursuit of sport which had preceded this final visit to the freshmarsh; a time to relax and enjoy the quietitude of the moment, with a mind unfettered by an urgent need to put a bird in the bag. Even though the marsh was empty, save for the dog and me, I did not feel alone because I knew that at this very moment fellow sportsmen nationwide would be experiencing similar emotions as they too enjoyed this final evening flight above the high tide mark. It is a wonderful yet sad moment in our sporting lives – indeed, there are few fitting comparisons.

With the light fading fast a scattering of floppy-winged lapwings came tumbling down to the flood, turning and wheeling this way and that so it was obvious that they were cautiously aware of my presence. At length they departed, and I heard them land a little way off, their calls coming loudly on the gentle breeze which now could scarcely find the strength to move the short grass stems at my feet. A partridge called somewhere behind me, to serve as a brief reminder of mild spring days to come, before silently settling down

Tufted love deeper waters.

for the night. Stars appeared overhead with increasing splendour, until the whole sky was all a-twinkle so that even the strengthening bite of the frost did little to mar the enjoyment of this most secret of moments. A mere glow remained in the west, and it was my task to concentrate on this patch of sky in an attempt to be ready should any late birds arrive.

With only the briefest of warnings a pair of mallard came to the flood on softly whispering wings, seeming huge and black against that western light. The drake fell with a splash into the shallows, whilst his mate turned quickly away and I did not fire – one was enough. Then the dog was away, racing through the water, scattering the thin layer of ice which had already begun to form, to bring the warm body to me. The drake was magnificent, resplendent in what would have been his breeding plumage a few weeks hence. In a few hours' time he could have come to this flood with impunity, but he had chosen to come this day and now he was dead – the dividing line between life and death can often be fine indeed.

The gloaming period had been overtaken by night: the day was all gone, so that the west lay black and devoid of any hint of light. I heard another party swish low overhead: then they were gone and I bade them farewell for another year, unless I should chance across them on the shore on the morrow.

A retrospective look at that evening flight is sadder still, for the tile-drainers have done their loathsome job well to ravage and ruin the marsh. Now cereal, or obscenely yellow oilseed rape, grows where once the cattle used to graze; the floods are no more, so the flight just described was the last enjoyed by any man on that marsh. The knowledge is sobering, but serves to heighten my enjoyment of a memory which, via this page, will endure for ever.

The wildfowler's dog

The wildfowler, be he the most lonesome soul in all creation, will generally be found in the company of at least one other – his dog. The astute reader will have noted my frequent reference to my own dog, albeit mostly in passing as though it was taken for granted. Indeed, there are no doubt times when we do take our canine partner for granted, for this is another typically human failing. The tyro might justifiably question the need for a dog at all, although experience will very soon negate any need for further elaboration. A dog is a good and faithful companion, most people would agree with this, and even if cats may be universally popular as household pets they can never aspire to the same high standards as our canine friends. Okay, so my own dog will be a companion, and even a friend in a loose sort of way, but first and foremost it will be the hired help, employed to do a specific job to the best of its ability – that being to retrieve any shot bird when bidden to do so.

Any man who takes up wildfowling as a sport without acquiring the services of a gundog is in line for a great deal of disappointment, for the business of consistently retrieving the shot quarry from the tangled saltmarsh or flooded creeks and tideways is something which should never be taken lightly. At times even a good dog will be hard-pressed to secure the bird when confronted with the most severe conditions of dark and cold and flood, whilst a wildfowler alone will have virtually no chance at all. Even in broad daylight a wounded duck will be remarkably adept at utilising the smallest scrap of cover, whilst even a duck which falls stone dead into the saltmarsh may never be seen again, for it is extraordinarily difficult to accurately mark the fall on an almost featureless marsh. Add the gloom of flight into the equation and the task of retrieval becomes almost impossible.

Water will be the biggest bane of all, for a wounded duck down in all but the shallowest water is capable of high-speed swimming and also has the ability to dive and resurface some considerable distance away. Even a good dog will have problems, so my strategy of an instant cripple-stopping shot at any wounded bird is a by-product of bitter experience and I heartily recommend this tactic to one and all. The dogless sportsman who shoots over water without either a dog of his own, or access to a dog close by will be hard put to effect a retrieve, and I personally doubt the ethics of shooting a bird which will not be gathered in. If you cannot retrieve the bird why shoot it in the first place? Far better to leave the bird for someone who is going to appreciate and respect it for the noble quarry which it undoubtedly is.

Geese are equally troublesome if not killed outright; indeed, add the ability to run at an amazing speed and retrieving duck may seem like child's play in comparison. Of course in an ideal world every shot will be perfectly delivered, with every bird dead in the air. But even the finest shot in the land will not be able to do this on every occasion, whilst the odd bird will remain unpicked, even despite the most strenuous of efforts. Anyone engaged in a lot of wildfowling who lays claim to having never lost a bird is something of a romantic. The wildfowling dog is perhaps one of the most loyal and long-suffering creatures currently in the service of Man. It will be asked to endure the sort of privation such as would horrify any dog lover, but will do so readily and eagerly, and be picture of

Yellow labrador.

abject misery should it be left at home for some reason or other. It will perform stout service, and even though many wildfowling dogs may be unruly brutes on occasion they are as important to the sport as the gun itself.

The traditional sporting picture of the wildfowler on the shore with a labrador at his side is well justified, for this breed is universally popular amongst devotees. Such popularity scarcely has any foundation in aesthetic appeal, but stems directly from an all-round suitability: the labrador is hardy, obedient, loyal and the possessor of almost infinite patience. They will mostly swim well, hunt competently – unless the cover is exceptionally dense – and retrieve gently to hand, whilst being powerful enough to handle the largest of grey geese. In short, the ideal wildfowling dog. Yet other breeds find favour, and I would be the last person to decry the choice of another. Spaniels are likely to be the choice of those with more than a passing interest in roughshooting, and I have known some springers that were superb wildfowling dogs, even if they were exceptionally unruly. I have noticed something of a trend toward German short-haired pointers of late and must say that they seem an excellent animal for this sort of work. But when all is said and done it is horses for courses, and the labrador is THE wildfowling dog. It is the traditional breed for the job and I do not see the tradition changing despite the modest inroads made by other, perhaps eminently suitable, breeds. Black or yellow it is all the same, with colour preferences being a question of individual taste: at present I run yellows, but have owned a black bitch in the past and would not hesitate to buy another at some future date.

The choice between dog or bitch is never clear-cut. A dog will be powerful and determined, but sometimes inclined to be a little headstrong. In contrast a bitch can be ultra-obedient and faithful, but often no less determined when confronted with a downed bird. Admittedly a bitch will have her two seasons a year, usually at the most inconvenient of times; but I have heard it said that a dog is in season all the year round! Perhaps there is some merit in the latter school of thought. Most certainly I have always owned bitches, and shall probably never change. I believe in sticking to a winning team, and for me a labrador bitch is a winner every time.

Final days

So to the shore for those final 20 hope-filled days. A strange, often dispiriting, time for the eager sportsman, for unless hard weather takes its toll there will be few duck to be had. The general ceasefire on the inland side of the seawall, occasioned by the end of the season, is sufficient to tempt many duck to loaf inland in this vast new-found sanctuary. Mallard in particular will be more interested in procreation than the normal business of flighting, whilst even the hosts of migrant ducks will seem curiously preoccupied. Only the grey geese seem to retain anything like their normal behaviour – although such normality amounts to a substantial problem for the wildfowler. So that February saw a relentless war of attrition against the geese, with a succession of long hikes to distant flighting places; of interminable vigils in the cold of the post-dusk night, and of crushing disappointments as the geese came through unscathed yet again. But any occasional success will be all the sweeter if it be well-earned, and there can be no doubt at all that any successes against the elusive white-fronted goose will be very well-earned indeed.

One of the most frustrating features of the goose hunt is their infuriating habit of sitting out in the fields long after they should have departed for their roost. But, as I mentioned earlier, everyone takes notice of what geese should do, except the geese themselves. On some days they will flight right on cue, whilst on others, even when conditions seem identical to us mere humans, they will flight very late indeed. Often I have sat in the saltings for hours after dark, in the vain hope that they will eventually flight, only for the flight to begin almost as soon as I pack up. Alternatively there has been no sound of them. One could quite easily spend all night skulking about in the saltings, waiting for the geese to flight; indeed, such a sacrifice would be well worthwhile if the geese eventually moved, but, of course, there can be no such guarantee. On balance I do not believe that I would want it to be otherwise, or else much of the magic of the chase would be lost. On those occasions when a small skein moves independently of the main flock it is well worth trying to call them within gunshot; mostly such a venture seems to fail, but success occurs often enough to make it a very viable proposition. As with other quarry, any calling should be carried out in a judicious manner, otherwise the whole affair will prove a waste of time. Call until you have the attention of the birds, then shut up before you alarm them.

That February was mostly inauspicious. The geese flighted erratically, with the presence of the moon largely to blame, whilst on the odd occasions when they did cross my section of shore they were mostly too high or too wide to warrant a shot. But perseverance often brings its own reward, and I was not left with absolutely nothing in return for my endeavours.

One evening towards the middle of the month I waited in a tacky mud hole on the edge of the saltings for the light to fade. The moon rose like a hopelessly lost waif to begin its journey across the night sky, and I knew that the geese would not leave their feeding grounds. Nevertheless, I waited on, but all to no avail – even though I stayed and froze for almost three hours after the western sky had turned black. At length I gave it best and trudged back into the firmer saltmarsh. Almost immediately the high-pitched yodel of white-fronts came to me on the chill night air, and although they passed fairly close they sounded very high indeed. Soon another skein came yelping out of the north, but this time they were much lower and I caught the vague glimpse of them as they swept past. Then, with ultimate cruelty, they swung ever lower over my mud hole before heading for the low tide mark. I called time and again, then, just when I thought I was wrecking my voice on some fruitless mission, they began to turn back in a long lazy arc over the shimmering moonlit mud until they were heading right for me. Strange how such an event can appear to be almost in slow motion: the painfully slow turn of the skein; the endless approach as they come beating up from the deep, and the rising crescendo of their voices calling urgently as they seek one of their number who has now fallen silent.

Then, all of a sudden, the great shapes are careering headlong into range, and there is just time to rise from the agonising crouch, raise the gun and fire. Then panic: one bird collapses, whilst the others cry out in alarm as they climb steeply for the stars above so that the second shot, with its split-second splash of bright flame, is a futile gesture at the fleeing forms. That goose was a magnificent adult bird – broad of breast and powerfully winged – struck down in the finest sporting tradition. I felt no remorse in the death, only a pride in my own achievement. In total contrast, a few days later a great storm had thrown itself spitefully upon the coast. It lay waste the saltings, so that barely a blade of *spartina* had withstood the fury, and thrashed the sea into a devil's cauldron of raging white water amongst which nothing could survive. I rushed to the shore in a state of high excitement, for surely, I reasoned, this would drive the geese from the fields, and with any luck within range of my waiting gun.

The tramp across the shore was even more unpleasant than usual, for the sky was massed over with sombre grey clouds whilst desperate sheets of rain swept the shore as though they attempted a futile escape from the unbridled fury of the storm. A great boat lay like some broken, drunken sea monster upon the mud where the storm had tossed it, the moorings were broken, whilst the hull lay at some crazy rakish angle, and the crew were wisely nowhere to be seen. At length I lay up in what I hoped would be a killing position, in the relative shelter of a deep creek as the gale raged insanely overhead as though intent on wiping this piece of shore from the face of the earth. Soon the light began to fade rapidly, and I knew that soon – in common with many such days – night would throw down its blackest cloak to blot out every hint of light.

A whisper of voices, staccato on the gale, came from the west to alert me that geese were on the move. But they must have quartered across me in the gloom unseen, for suddenly on a huge blast of wind I heard their mad, cackling laughter telling me that they were past. Then they were gone off to the east, to the safety of some secret goose roost of sighing wings and white-tipped goose droppings.

Almost immediately more undulating voices from the west told of more geese heading my way. But I could scarcely bear to look in that direction as the rain came in great stinging droplets that threatened to blind me if I did not cower from their fury. A ragged, wind-blown skein came across the wind at incredible speed and I had only a split-second to decide whether or not they were worthy of a shot; shamefully, I cowered from the rain, and in that hesitation they were gone. The doubt and the uncertainty were there, and remain with me still, but pose questions which I can never answer. The geese had gone, and darkness came with a crushing finality to blot out every glimmer of light – save for a couple of man-made pin-pricks in the distance to remind me that I was not the last man alive. Now the return trip in true darkness, a trip which became a fearful nightmare of slippery-sided gutters, and uneven, hard-packed mud which was eager to send me over at each step. In this it succeeded with unpleasant regularity.

Gradually I became aware of a flash of light somewhere behind me, lighting the salting ahead briefly, and I realised instantly, with utmost trepidation, what it was. To a lonely, rain-soaked figure on a flat featureless saltmarsh the prospect of lightning is daunting in the extreme. The next flash lit up the whole shore in a sudden blaze of white light – the storm-blasted salting, the near-horizontal driving rain, and the somehow sinister hulk on the mud. Instantly the salting was plunged into total all-consuming blackness, the conditions were even worse than before, with me being quite dazed and blinded. The next strike was very close, with the drunken hulk now taking on horror film proportions so that I could imagine some ghoulish black-caped figure lurking in the darkness somewhere up ahead! But the threat from the storm was the real danger, and I accepted it as such: the impulse to lay aside my lightning conductor of a gun and distance myself from it was strong, but I resisted it – although to this day I do not know whether I behaved wisely or not.

Yet the lightning was soon gone off to the east, so that its disturbing presence no longer interrupted the consistency of the blackout, leaving me to pick my way back to a car which lay glistening under the storm. The storm had penetrated my clothing to a degree but, apart from the fright, I was none the worse, so a hot bath and meal soon prepared me for another dose of the same if the need arose!

The final day

So the final day of the season had arrived. One more try for the geese, more out of a sense of duty than through any realistic hope of a shot, for duty calls on the last day of the season as surely as it does on the first. Regardless of sporting prospects the call of the geese is irresistable to so many, and I for one am loathe to even attempt to break its grip. It was a typical end-of-season day, being both mild and calm making it easy to imagine that spring was indeed just around the corner. The shore seemed peaceful, almost idyllic, and but for the severe storm damage it would have been difficult to tell exactly what time of the year it was. There were few birds on the shore, save for some amorously displaying shelduck and a sprinkling of waders, whilst only a great cloud of buzzing brent geese and a few very high wigeon showed themselves at dusk. There is a kind of sadness attached to that final moment when the sun slides out of sight below the western horizon, to leave the redness of its passing as a reminder of all those other sunsets throughout the season past. Slowly the redness fades, and I feel winter fade and die with it. The season will have been long and hard, but frequently memorable in its make-up. I like so many of my kind, feel the loss: I grieve for the lost sport and for the lost magic of the shore, for, although the shore will always remain, the loss of sport somehow detracts from the magnificence of the place. I left without sight nor sound of the geese. How mean of them, I mused, on the long trudge back. But at the death they flighted further up the coast, so that for a little while the air was filled with their wondrously wild calling. I could thus go home duly satisfied that the geese and I had said our fond farewells, without alarm or the spilling of blood – perhaps it should always be this way on the last day.

Yes, perhaps almost six months of intensive wildfowling is as

185

much as the flesh and blood can stand. In any case the summer will be gone again quickly enough, and it will soon be time to get down onto the shore again in pursuit of the wildfowl, and even if the bag be small the enjoyment will invariably be beyond price. The wheel will turn full circle, as it must, and winter will begin again. The chase too will once again be on, and man and dog and wily birds will again become locked in an endless struggle which is as old as time itself; if we are left be it will always be this way for the lonesome wildfowler on his lonely shore, engaged in his timeless contest with the elements and some of Nature's wildest spirits.

The ways of the shore and its inhabitants will change but little, if left in peace. Only Man can dictate the pace of life and change on the shores and coasts, and with luck he will have learnt recent lessons well. Perhaps at the final reckoning we shall be left in peace to enjoy the shore and our wildfowling ways.

> Away to the west the sun,
> Set in its dying glow,
> Slides peacefully to sleep.
> How many eyes watch?
> How many hearts cry out
> For these peaceful primitive hours?

Away to the east lies the sea,
Grey and quivering; murmuring
As a lightly sleeping babe.
A great gull booms:
The vast mudflat is his,
Who would challenge or disturb him?

Up above an inky sky,
Filled with a host of twinkling stars,
Begins to lay its canopy:
Of darkness; of cold; of unspoken fears.
A canopy that hides all evil,
And all good alike.
The world seems at peace
As darkness spreads its giant hands
And enfolds man, dog and salting;
Enfolds the mudflats, the great gull,
And the setting sun.

What will come this frosty night,
To feed upon this wide saltmarsh?
To dibble in its pools,
And splash and preen
Before the dawn.

A tiny snipe, hurrying,
On slender quicksilver wings,
Dives past to its nightly feed.
To probe, with long straight bill,
The soft nutritious muds
To fill its tiny gut.

Now darkness is complete.
No snipe to join that lonely snipe;
No geese to inflame the senses;
No sound of whistling wings
Or stuttering mallard's call –
No matter.

A. L. JARRETT